PSYCHOLOGY RESEARCH PROGRESS

TRAIT AND STATE ANXIETY

ASSESSMENT, PREDICTORS AND OUTCOMES

PSYCHOLOGY RESEARCH PROGRESS

Additional books in this series can be found on Nova's website
under the Series tab.

Additional e-books in this series can be found on Nova's website
under the eBooks tab.

HUMAN ANATOMY AND PHYSIOLOGY

Additional books in this series can be found on Nova's website
under the Series tab.

Additional e-books in this series can be found on Nova's website
under the eBooks tab.

PSYCHOLOGY RESEARCH PROGRESS

TRAIT AND STATE ANXIETY

ASSESSMENT, PREDICTORS AND OUTCOMES

ABEL BRADLEY
EDITOR

nova publishers
New York

NOTICE TO THE READER

Library of Congress Cataloging-in-Publication Data

Library of Congress Control Number: 2016933393

ISBN: 978-1-63484-840-4

Published by Nova Science Publishers, Inc. † New York

Contents

PREFACE

Anxiety can be defined as an emotional state that combines either physiological and psychological response and reflects a stage of cognitive and behavioral alert that an organism mobilizes in response to a potential distress. This pathology can be conceptualized as having two components: state and trait. Trait anxiety refers to an individual's personality and predisposition for anxiety, whereas state anxiety refers to the emotional response generated by a perceived distress. This book provides current research on the assessment, predictors and outcomes of trait and state anxiety. Chapter One examines the "Spielberger State – Trait Anxiety Inventory" (STAI) as a tool for assessing trait and state anxiety. Chapter Two provides an overview of the development of anxiety, reviews the available literature on state and trait anxiety, including the neuroanatomical correlates, and presents a collective overview of cognition and the aging brain, with emphasis on the specific impact of anxiety on this process. Chapter Three provides a brief description of Attention Deficit with Hyperactivity Disorder (ADHD), with a focus on comorbidity between ADHD and anxiety disorders, and examines the concept of anxiety and the different classifications of the disorder in relation to the most commonly-utilized assessment methods and instruments at the present time. The final chapter, Chapter Four, studies the possible existence of gender differences in sleep organization of individuals with low and high trait anxiety levels.

Chapter 1 - Anxiety can be defined as an emotional state that combines either physiological and psychological response and reflects a stage of cognitive and behavioral alert that an organism mobilizes in response to a potential distress. This pathology can be conceptualized as having two components: state and trait. Trait anxiety refers to an individual's personality and predisposition for anxiety, whereas state anxiety refers to the emotional response generated by a perceived distress. In this way, the "Spielberger State – Trait Anxiety Inventory" (STAI) is composed of two different scales for measuring these two concepts of anxiety. This inventory is comprised of 20 items and composed of two different 4-point Likert-type scales designed to measure state anxiety (part I) and trait anxiety (part II); each item has 4 response options scored 0 (never/almost never) to 3 (always/almost always). thus the range of possible scores on each subscale is 20 (low anxiety) to 80 (high anxiety). In the both questionnaires some items are reverse-coded, in the STAI-S they are 1, 2, 5, 8, 10, 11, 15, 16, 19, 20; and in the STAI-T 1, 3, 6, 7, 10, 13, 14, 16, 19. Higher scores on both scales indicate more anxiety symptoms. Scores on the STAI-S and STAI-T ≥ 30 suggest moderate anxiety and scores ≥ 45 suggest severe anxiety according to the authors, however there are some studies that utilized different count-points.

Chapter 2 - Research suggests that psychopathological disorders can have specific impacts on cognitive functioning (e.g., slower processing speed in those with depression); however, there is less information about the impact of anxiety on the aging brain. In addition to providing an overview of the development of anxiety (i.e., epidemiology, prevalence, risk factors), this chapter will review the available literature on state and trait anxiety, including the neuroanatomical correlates. Authors will then present a collective overview of cognition and the aging brain, with emphasis on the specific impact of anxiety on this process. For example, many studies have found that higher levels of state anxiety have been associated with impaired learning and poor memory performance in older adults, while trait anxiety has been positively correlated with deficits in attention; however, little research has concluded how these systemically relate. As such, particular focus will be placed on the implications associated with onset and duration of anxiety symptomatology and its overall effect on the risk of developing cognitive decline, including mild cognitive impairment and dementia. Additionally, current treatment modalities for cognitive training and physical health will be reviewed and implemented.

Chapter 3 - Attention Deficit with Hyperactivity Disorder (ADHD) is one of the most prevalent disorders in childhood and affects about 5% of school students. ADHD is characterized by three main symptoms: inattention, hyperactivity and impulsivity. These deficits suggest a problem in the voluntary control of behavior that is generally associated with executive functioning impairments (e.g., deficits in working memory, planning, organization, concentration, and cognitive flexibility). Moreover, ADHD is frequently accompanied by different disorders, especially anxiety, which is present in 20% to 50% of ADHD cases. This comorbidity usually has important effects on the expression of ADHD deficits in both children and adolescents. Thus, it is necessary to systematically examine the potential consequences of this association. The primary goals of this study are to firstly carry out an exhaustive review of previous research on this topic, and thereafter analyze executive function profiles in a cohort of students with ADHD and anxiety (aged 6 to 16 years). In order to clearly describe the findings and results of these goals, the present chapter comprises the following structure: 1) A brief introduction describing ADHD and executive functions deficits, with a particular focus on comorbidity between ADHD and anxiety disorders; 2) The concept of anxiety and the different classifications of this disorder is discussed in relation to the most commonly-utilized assessment methods and instruments at the present time; 3) The implications of the presence of anxiety on executive deficits in ADHD are explained, and then examined in the light of an empirical study involving a small sample of students with these very characteristics (comorbid ADHD and anxiety disorders); 4) The results from this analysis are then discussed, and some practical implications are also presented. The aspects addressed in the present chapter will provide readers with an initial insight into this problematic aspect of ADHD, and its important consequences concerning children and adolescent individuals and their future academic achievement.

Chapter 4 - One hundred and ten healthy volunteers, men and women undergraduates from 19 to 25 years of age took part in preliminary survey. According to survey data sixty four participants with low and high trait anxiety completed one night of home-based polysomnography, the sleep structure was drawn and electroencephalography analysis was done. The shorter sleep duration, more time awake, less delta-sleep and less REM stage without signs of subsequent compensation were found among individuals of high trait anxiety. In addition to that the lower theta power in high anxious men and lower delta power, higher alpha and beta powers in anxious women in delta-sleep were obtained. The lower theta power in REM stage for anxious individuals was displayed. As a result, an anxious women are more vulnerable to the sleep disturbances than anxious men.

In: Trait and State Anxiety
Editor: Abel Bradley

ISBN: 978-1-63484-840-4

Chapter 1

The Spielberger Inventory Like a Tool for Assess the Trait and State Anxiety

Caroline Ronchini Ferreira and Roberta Ribeiro Silva
Faculdade de Nutrição, Universidade Federal de Alfenas (UNIFAL-MG), Rua Gabriel Monteiro da Silva, Alfenas, MG, Brazil

Abstract

Anxiety can be defined as an emotional state that combines either physiological and psychological response and reflects a stage of cognitive and behavioral alert that an organism mobilizes in response to a potential distress. This pathology can be conceptualized as having two components: state and trait. Trait anxiety refers to an individual's personality and predisposition for anxiety, whereas state anxiety refers to the emotional response generated by a perceived distress. In this way, the "Spielberger State – Trait Anxiety Inventory" (STAI) is composed of two different scales for measuring these two concepts of anxiety. This inventory is comprised of 20 items and composed of two different 4-point Likert-type scales designed to measure state anxiety (part I) and trait anxiety (part II); each item has 4 response options scored 0 (never/almost never) to 3 (always/almost always). thus the range of possible scores on each subscale is 20 (low anxiety) to 80 (high anxiety). In the both questionnaires some items are reverse-coded, in the STAI-S they are 1, 2, 5, 8, 10, 11, 15, 16, 19, 20; and in the STAI-T 1, 3, 6, 7, 10, 13, 14, 16, 19. Higher scores on both scales indicate more anxiety symptoms. Scores on the STAI-S and STAI-T ≥ 30 suggest moderate anxiety and scores ≥ 45 suggest severe anxiety according to the authors, however there are some studies that utilized different count-points.

TRAIT AND STATE ANXIETY: ASSESSMENT, PREDICTORS AND OUTCOMES

Anxiety can be defined as a feeling of agitation and restlessness in response to certain situations that combines both physiological and psychological reactions. Is often triggered by feelings of fear in the face of imminent danger and reflects a state of cognitive and behavioral preparedness that an organism mobilizes in response to a potential threat. Is characterized by a feeling of unease, nervousness, or worry about an event with an uncertain outcome. These subjective symptoms are often accompanied by physiological signs of excitation, such as sweating, trembling, dizziness or a rapid heartbeat.

Occasional anxiety is a normal part of life, but can become pathological or a disorder when it is frequent or chronic and begins to interfere with daily activities such as work, school, and relationships. Anxiety disorders involve more than temporary worry or fear, this means that for a person with an anxiety disorder, the anxiety does not go away and can get worse over time. There are a diversity of anxiety disorders, which jointly, are among the most common mental disorder.

According to the European Study of the Epidemiology of Mental Disorders (ESEMeD), 13.6% of the population has lived some type of anxiety disorder at one point in their lives. Generally, the prevalence rates range from 15% to 52% for anxiety symptoms and 3% to 15% for clinical anxiety disorders that match diagnostic guidelines.

Specifically, from the neurological point of view, anxiety can be rated as state or trait dependent.

State anxiety is a transitory emotional state that consists of feelings of apprehension and tension experienced in a particular stressful situation and characterized by consciously perceived subjective feelings of tension and apprehension, this state varies in intensity and fluctuates over time, being associated with heightened activity of the autonomic nervous system.

Trait anxiety is an uninterrupted personality trait, that is, an individual tendency to perceive stressful situations as threatening, which in turn increases the individual's level of anxiety, that is, is a constant psychological characteristic, that makes a person susceptible to chronic anxiety.

In this way, the "Spielberger State – Trait Anxiety Inventory" (STAI) is composed of two different theoretical model that recognizes these two concepts of anxiety, being a commonly used instrument for measuring anxiety in adults. The STAI differentiates between the temporary condition of state anxiety and the more general and long-standing quality of trait anxiety.

Either of these two components is assessed with a 20-item self-reported subscale, scored on a four-point Likert-type scale, each item has 4 response options scored 0 (never/almost never) to 3 (always/almost always), thus the range of possible scores on each subscale is 20 (low anxiety) to 80 (high anxiety). In the STAI State the subjects being asked to respond based on "how you feel right now" and in the STAI Trait subjects being asked to respond based on "how you generally feel."

Originally, the STAI form was constructed by Charles D. Spielberger, Richard L. Gorsuch, and Robert E. Lushene in 1964. The STAI has been adapted in more than 30 languages for cross-cultural research and clinical practice.

The essential qualities evaluated by the STAI are feelings of apprehension, tension, nervousness, and worry. The reliability coefficient (Cronbach's a), referring to a normative sample of men and women, is 0.91 for STAI State and 0.90 for STAI Trait.

The STAI is the most commonly validated self-report questionnaire used how assessment tool for the experience of anxiety related to stress, differentiating between the situational experience and the overarching predisposition toward stress or anxiety with the "State'' and "Trait" subscales. It has been widely used for > 40 years and has validated norms in the general population and a variety of patient populations.

Various reliability and validity tests have been conducted on the STAI and have provided sufficient evidence that the STAI is an appropriate and adequate measure for studying anxiety in research and clinical settings.

The state and trait anxiety scores can be directly computed as the sum of scores of each item and have a direct interpretation: high scores on their respective scales mean more trait or state anxiety and low scores mean less anxiety level. In the both questionnaires some items are reverse-coded, in the STAI State they are 1, 2, 5, 8, 10, 11, 15, 16, 19, 20; and in the STAI Trait 1, 3, 6, 7, 10, 13, 14, 16, 19. Total score on each subscale was the sum of all item scores (negatively-keyed items were reverse-scored).

In this way, higher scores on both scales indicate more anxiety symptoms, according to the authors, scores ≥ 30 suggest moderate anxiety and scores ≥ 45 suggest severe anxiety, however there are some studies that utilized different count-points.

References

Dumont, Y.; Quirion, R. 2014. Neuropeptide Y Pathways in Anxiety-Related Disorders. *Biol Psychiatry* 76:834–835.

Fernández-Blázquez, M.A.; Ávila-Villanueva, M.; López-Pina, J.A.; Zea-Sevilla, M.A.; Frades-Payo, B. 2015. Psychometric properties of a new short version of the State-Trait Anxiety Inventory (STAI) for the assessment of anxiety in the elderly. *Neurología* 30(6):352-358.

Mah, L.; Szabuniewicz, C.; Fiocco, A.J. 2016. Can anxiety damage the brain? *Curr Opin Psychiatry* 29(1):56–63.

Meltzer-Brody, S.; Zerwas, S.; Leserman, J.; Von Holle, A.; Regis, T.; Bulik, C. 2011. Eating Disorders and Trauma History in Women with Perinatal Depression. *Journal of Women's Health* 20(6):863-870.

Qiu, A.; Rifkin-Graboi, A.; Chen, H.; Chong, Y.S.; Kwek, K.; Gluckman, P.D.; Fortier, M.V.; Meaney, M.J. 2013. Maternal anxiety and infants' hippocampal development: timing matters. *Translational Psychiatry* 3:1-7.

Silva, N.C.F.; Silva, B.R.; Vasconcelos, H.M.; Oliveira, P.M.C.; Teixeira, E.H.; Aguiar, A.S.W. 2015. Profile of brazilian dental students and its relationship to anxiety levels. *Rev Med UFC* 55(1):25-32.

Turner, K.; Reynolds-May, M.F.; Zitek, E.M.; Tisdale, R.L.; Carlisle, A.B.; Westphal, L.M. 2013. Stress and Anxiety Scores in First and Repeat IVF Cycles: A Pilot Study. *Plos One* 8(5):1-6.

In: Trait and State Anxiety
Editor: Abel Bradley
ISBN: 978-1-63484-840-4

Chapter 2

DIFFERENTIATING THE IMPACT OF STATE VERSUS TRAIT ANXIETY ON COGNITIVE FUNCTIONING OF THE AGING BRAIN

Cory E. Harrison[1,2,*], Pavel Litvin[1,3], Rachel Lavian[1,4], Suranee A. Waleszonia[1] and Karen J. Miller[1,†]

[1]University of California, Los Angeles,
Semel Institute for Neuroscience and Human Behavior,
Longevity Center, California, Los Angeles, US
[2]Azusa Pacific University, Department of Graduate Psychology,
Azusa, California, US
[3]Fielding Graduate University, Department of Psychology,
Santa Barbara, California, US
[4]Alliant University, Department of Psychology,
San Diego, California, US

* Manuscript correspondence: Cory E. Harrison, M.A.; Division of Geriatric Psychiatry, David Geffen School of Medicine, UCLA; Semel Institute for Neuroscience & Human Behavior; Longevity Center, Suite 3119; Peter V. Ueberroth Building; 10945 Le Conte Avenue; Los Angeles, CA 90095-6980; charrison@mednet.ucla.edu.

† Manuscript correspondence: Karen J. Miller, Ph.D.; Division of Geriatric Psychiatry, David Geffen School of Medicine, UCLA; Semel Institute for Neuroscience & Human Behavior; Longevity Center, Suite 3119; Peter V. Ueberroth Building; 10945 Le Conte Avenue; Los Angeles, CA 90095-6980; kmiller@mednet.ucla.edu.

Abstract

Research suggests that psychopathological disorders can have specific impacts on cognitive functioning (e.g., slower processing speed in those with depression); however, there is less information about the impact of anxiety on the aging brain. In addition to providing an overview of the development of anxiety (i.e., epidemiology, prevalence, risk factors), this chapter will review the available literature on state and trait anxiety, including the neuroanatomical correlates. Authors will then present a collective overview of cognition and the aging brain, with emphasis on the specific impact of anxiety on this process. For example, many studies have found that higher levels of state anxiety have been associated with impaired learning and poor memory performance in older adults, while trait anxiety has been positively correlated with deficits in attention; however, little research has concluded how these systemically relate. As such, particular focus will be placed on the implications associated with onset and duration of anxiety symptomatology and its overall effect on the risk of developing cognitive decline, including mild cognitive impairment and dementia. Additionally, current treatment modalities for cognitive training and physical health will be reviewed and implemented.

Introduction

Despite the prevalence of anxiety in older adults, little is known about the psychopathological features as it occurs in the geriatric population. Researchers have come to acknowledge that anxiety consists of two separable components: state anxiety, which refers to a temporary emotional reaction; and trait anxiety, which refers to a relatively stable personality disposition. In addition, studies have shown that each of these can exacerbate cognitive decline, as seen in the aging brain. This understanding is central to the practice of healthy aging, and becomes essential in treating both neurocognitive decline and comorbid psychological disorders. Over the course of this chapter, we will define both anxiety and cognitive functioning as they relate to the geriatric population, including the continuum of neurocognitive decline in the course of normal aging and age-related conditions, including mild cognitive disorder and dementia. We will then delve into the structural and functional changes of the aging brain, and explain their role in mood regulation and cognitive functioning. This will be followed with the differentiation of state and trait anxiety, which includes how cognition and overall functioning in the aging population are affected. Finally, we will review a variety of methods to treat and manage anxiety as they relate to cognitive training and health.

DEFINING ANXIETY

Anxiety is an emotion characterized by a surge of activity in a specific location in the brain (HPA axis; to be defined in later sections), which causes psychological discomfort ranging from slight uneasiness to immobilizing fear (Scrable, Burns-Cusato and Medrano, 2009). Common to many individuals, feelings of anxiety can be considered normal when experienced under stressful situations and in short duration (Barisa, 2014; Scrable et al., 2009); however, some people experience anxious emotional activity for elongated periods of time and/or under inappropriate circumstances (Scrable et al., 2009). In humans, prevalence rates can be as high as 8% of the overall population (Scrable et al., 2009); however in older adults anxiety symptoms can occur as often as 20% (Barisa, 2014; Rodda, Boyce and Walker, 2008).

Anxiety is experienced as a part of everyday life and can be viewed along a continuum; mild anxiety is noted to improve productivity and motivation, while intense anxiety promotes survival skills essential in response to danger (Barisa, 2014). However, when anxiety occurs during inappropriate times or becomes excessive and interferes with daily life, it may be clinically diagnosed as an anxiety disorder (Barisa, 2014). As such, clinical anxiety can affect people on a physiological, behavioral, and psychological level (Barisa, 2014). Common symptoms include muscle tension, rapid heart rate, sweating, trembling in hands or wobbliness in legs, gastrointestinal discomfort, headaches, dizziness, shortness of breath, choking sensations, sleep disturbance, emotional arousal, and cognitive complaints (Barisa, 2014; Beck, Stanley and Zebb, 1996).

STATE AND TRAIT ANXIETY

In 1966, Spielberger suggested a more clearly defined concept of anxiety in which the disorder should be introduced as multifaceted and with a distinction between trait anxiety and state anxiety (Spielberger, Gorsuch and Lushene, 1970). According to Spielberger (1970) anxiety should be considered as both a temporary emotional state, commonly experienced (state anxiety) and a consistent personality attribute (trait anxiety). More simply put, trait anxiety can be viewed as the person's natural default demeanor, whereas state anxiety can be viewed as a person's reaction to a specific situation.

Trait Anxiety

Trait anxiety refers to a phenomenon that is distinguished from common bouts of anxious feelings and is more chronic in nature. Additionally, it has a longer duration, with symptoms persisting for months to years, and is described as a personality disposition (Bourne, 2005; Teachman, 2006). Trait based anxiety is assessed by analyzing the predisposition to experience anxiety in the following situations: social evaluation, physical danger, ambiguous, and daily routines (Endler & Kocovski, 2001). Trait anxiety can therefore be identified by the following criteria: anxious responses are greater in proportion and experienced in a greater variety of situations; the number and intensity of anxious responses; duration of anxious responses; and the fearfulness evoked in situations (Endler & Kocovski, 2001).

The classical definition of trait anxiety implies a generalized and long-standing predisposition to react to many and most situations in a consistently anxious manner (Endler & Kocovski, 2001). This assumes that trait anxiety is more inherent in nature, and refers to the rather persistent tendency in an individual to respond with state anxiety to a perceived or potential threat (Spielberger et al., 1970). More recently, it has been argued that trait anxiety also remains multidimensional and can include the following four facets: social evaluation, physical danger, ambiguity, and daily routines (Endler & Kocovski, 2001).

Additionally, trait anxiety is not directly manifested in behavior but can be inferred by how frequently a person experiences state-based anxiety over time (Reiss, 1997). Trait theorists believe in individual differences, meaning that each person will respond and express stress and/or anxiety in unique ways (Endler & Kocovski, 2001). However, while no theorist accepts the concept of absolute consistency (e.g., a person behaves at the same level of anxiety at all times), most support the notion of relative consistency (e.g., an anxious person will experience symptoms of anxiety across most situations) (Endler & Kocovski, 2001).

An example of trait anxiety would include a similar response to all medical appointments (i.e., equally afraid of a routine appointment with the primary care physician, the dentist, or a general practitioner) in which the potential threat may be real or imagined. The same could be said for fear of certain social situations (i.e., attending a party), or crowded events. In addition, some people with high levels of trait anxiety may experience anxious feelings in various situations that do not evoke anxiety in most people; examples include crossing a street intersection or shopping at a grocery store. The trait anxiety would be a life-long expression of worry, as well as a constant stressful response to most situations.

State Anxiety

When anxiety occurs in the context of shorter durations (minutes or hours) or in response to a specific threat, and dissipates as the threat weakens, it is considered to be state anxiety. As aforementioned, state anxiety is ". . . an emotional state or condition which is characterized by subjective feelings of tension, apprehension, and worry, and by activation or arousal of the autonomic nervous system" (Magnusson, 1980, p. 215). State anxiety can also be classified in terms of observable behaviors, cognitive symptomatology, and physiological events (Reiss, 1997).

Similarly, state anxiety has also been argued as multidimensional in which two facets, cognitive-worry and autonomic-emotional (Endler & Kocovski, 2001) are considered. Cognitive-worry is commonly perceived as the pervasive thoughts and distorted thinking, where as autonomic-emotional can be viewed as the psychosomatic symptoms. For example, older adults may develop worry or stress related to perceived cognitive decline and the possible consequences (e.g., loss of driver's license, the development of dementia, the need to depend on their children). Subsequently, they may develop certain behavioral responses. This can be developed in the form of either cognitive worry (e.g., obsessively signing up for cognitive training classes or reading books on how to improve memory) or autonomic emotional responses (e.g., increased irritability or tearfulness when experiencing a reminder of the cognitive decline).

State anxiety is viewed as an unpleasant emotion, which precipitates variable reactions of an individual's variables in interaction with specific situational stressors (Endler, Kantor and Parker, 1994). An individual may attempt to change the aversive nature of state anxiety by using specific coping responses (Endler et al., 1994). Research has identified two areas of coping responses: emotion-focused (person-oriented) and problem-focused (task oriented) coping strategies (Endler et al., 1994). A third coping strategy, avoidance, has also been identified, which can be expressed in both task or person oriented strategies (Endler et al., 1994). Coping preferences used by an individual may then impact how that individual will behave under stress. For example, consider a person, who experiences state-based anxiety surrounding public speaking. An emotion-focused response may include deep breathing exercises or talk-therapy, whereas a problem-focused response would be to rehearse the speech several times prior or participate in a public speaking class or seminar; an avoidance response would include avoiding all speaking engagements. Research has hypothesized that state anxiety can be predicted by the specific coping strategies of the individual (Endler et al., 1994), as opposed to existing theories that have suggested trait anxiety as the sole predictor of state based symptoms (Magnusson, 1980). As such, late-life anxiety and/or situational stressors can be further examined under the correlate of state anxiety as it appears in the geriatric population.

ANXIETY WITHIN THE GERIATRIC POPULATION

While anxiety disorders are more commonly diagnosed in younger populations, research still estimates that approximately 20% of the older adult population may experience anxiety symptoms (Scrable et al., 2009). This is increased by an additional 10% in the medically ill population (Beck et al., 1996); additionally, approximately 23.5% of caregivers (often older adults caring for spouses) experience anxiety (Bryant, Jackson and Ames, 2008). As for trait versus state anxiety in older adults, it has been documented that approximately 3.7-7.4% of older adults have dealt with life-long struggles of anxiety (characterized here as trait anxiety; (Scrable et al., 2009), while 24.4% of older adults experience late-life manifestations (state anxiety) at some point after the age of 55 (Bryant et al., 2008; Rodda et al., 2008). As such, the prevalence of anxiety disorders (trait-based) is much lower than that of anxiety symptoms (state-based) (Bryant et al., 2008), and will be an important clarification for treatment.

Possible causes of anxiety in older adults may include: social isolation, decreased autonomy, financial insecurity, poor health, and impending death, all of which can increase prevalence of anxiety in late life (Flint, 1994). Anxiety causes considerable subjective distress (Bryant et al., 2008), reduced life satisfaction (Brenes et al., 2005), and increases the risk of disability and mortality (Beck et al., 1996; Bryant et al., 2008). The typical symptoms of anxiety for older adults include: impaired sleep, memory and attention impairment, ruminative/pervasive thoughts, repetitive behaviors, agitation, persistent worry, avoidance of certain settings, and several autonomic signs (e.g., shortness of breath, tightness in chest, headaches, heart palpitations, sweating) (Bryant et al., 2008; Cassidy & Rector, 2008; Rodda et al., 2008). Unlike the solitary anxiety disorder seen in younger individuals, anxiety in older adults is often co-morbid with medical illness or depression, and there is substantial overlap in symptoms (Cassidy & Rector, 2008).

Associated cognitive symptoms of underlying anxiety disorders include hypervigilance, increased vulnerability, and perceiving the demands of life as exceeding the available resources to cope (Cassidy & Rector, 2008). As such, older adults are at a higher risk due to increasing frailty, medical illness, and losses (e.g., loss of ability, death of loved ones, loss of independence) – all of which can contribute to feelings of fear potentially activating anxiety disorders (Cassidy & Rector, 2008). Additional risk factors include, lack of social support, diagnosis of cognitive decline, recent traumatic events, medical illness and medications, poor self-rated health, comorbid psychiatric illness (e.g., depression, another anxiety disorder), dysfunctional coping strategies, and female gender (Cassidy & Rector, 2008; Vink, Aartsen and Schoevers, 2008).

Anxiety disorders encompass a variety of conditions, including panic disorder, phobias, post-traumatic stress disorder, and generalized anxiety disorder (Teachman, 2006). The most common form of anxiety in the older adult is generalized anxiety disorder (GAD), which is characterized by at least 6 months of anxious feelings accompanied by symptoms of motor tension, vigilance, perseveration, and rumination. Approximately 20% of older adults will experience GAD at least once in their life (Cassidy & Rector, 2008; Rodda et al., 2008), often within the co-morbidity of other psychiatric disorders, including depression, physical illness, and dementia (Barisa, 2014; Booth, Schinka, Brown, Mortimer and Borenstein, 2006; Teachman, 2006). Research indicates that GAD in older adults is often characterized by heightened reports of worry, generalized anxiety, social fears, and depressed mood (Beck et al., 1996).

Additionally, recent studies have shown that specific phobias represent up to 80% of new-onset anxiety cases in older adults (Cassidy & Rector, 2008). Unlike younger adults, specific phobias in older adults do not always accompany panic disorders, but typically follow traumatic events such as medical illness, death of a spouse, or a fall (Cassidy & Rector, 2008). Collectively, for older adults living independently, anxiety is noted to surpass other late-life diagnoses; being twice as common as dementia (8%) and major depression (1-3%) (Cassidy & Rector, 2008; Cole & Dendukuri, 2003). Note that for older adults major depression occurs in 1-3% of the general population, and an additional 8-16% experience clinically significant depressive symptoms (Cole & Dendukuri, 2003). Moreover, with seniors who are living in nursing homes, the rate of anxiety and depression increases, with approximately 14-20% suffering from a mood disorder (Byers, Yaffe, Covinsky, Friedman and Bruce, 2010). Even with high prevalence rates, anxiety continues to be misdiagnosed and under-treated in the geriatric population (Ayers, Sorrell, Thorp and Wetherell, 2007).

Recent research suggests anxiety remains particularly neglected, due to a consistent view that anxiety simply co-occurs with depression (Bryant et al., 2008). However, research states that the prevalence of mixed anxiety and depression is significantly lower than either disorder alone (Wetherell, Gatz and Craske, 2003). In fact, anxiety disorders are 4 to 7 times more prevalent than major depression in older adults (Beck, 1995; Wolitzky-Taylor, Castriotta, Lenze, Stanley and Craske, 2010); currently, at least 14% of older adults experience at least one episode of anxiety after the age of 55 (Wolitzky-Taylor et al., 2010), but only an estimate of 4% of older adults after the age of 55 (who are living independently) experience an episode of depression, with a higher prevalence among women (Beekman et al., 1995; Blazer, 2002). Additionally, their anxiety may be overlooked in the context of normal bereavement or grief (Barisa, 2014). Collectively, this suggests a need to better represent anxiety in the geriatric population for better and more complete treatment.

Overview of Neuroanatomy and Neuroendocrinology Involved

In this section, we will explore neuroendocrine (i.e., systems involved in the regulation of hormones) and neuroanatomical (i.e., brain regions and networks) processes involved in the psychological constructs of state and trait anxiety. It should be noted that the following is an abbreviated version of the complex interdependent interaction between sensory, physiologic, and subcortical and cortical systems involved in anxiety. For a more comprehensive review, see Charney (2003).

Briefly, neuroimaging, electrophysiological, and lesion analyses studies of both animals and humans have implicated several interdependent brain structures related to acquiring and maintaining anxiety states and traits, including the amygdala, a number of mesiotemporal cortical structures, the sensory thalamus and cortices, the orbital and medial prefrontal cortex, the anterior insula, the hypothalamus, and multiple brainstem nuclei. Additionally, a robust body of research suggests the involvement of the hypothalamic-pituitary-adrenal (HPA) axis as one of the most salient neuronal and neuroendocrine systems related to the management of anxiety, since it is responsible for secreting and regulating stress hormones that prepare the body to face a threat. Overall, state anxiety is a transitory state typically involving the amygdala (i.e., the brain's fear center) and HPA axis activation (i.e., release of stress hormones in response to a threat), while trait anxiety is likely related to dysfunction in the "calming" or modulating systems (i.e., processes that aim to keep and bring the body to resting state) within the neocortex and HPA axis.

With regard to older adults, this population naturally experiences increased sensitivity to anxious states (i.e., more frequent release of stress hormones via the HPA axis) in addition to experiencing a decline in the growth of new neuronal cells that help manage anxious states. Additionally, neurotoxic consequences (i.e., neuronal cell death) can occur more rapidly if older adults are chronically exposed to stress, which further reduces modulating (i.e., calming) systems in HPA axis that aim to bring the older adult back to a homeostatic non-anxious state. Thus, if these HPA axis "calming" systems perform poorly, states of anxiety are expected to occur more frequently in older adults, which incidentally further damages these "calming" systems; this downward spiral of reduced ability to regulate anxious states can lead to a tendency to view the world as threatening (i.e., trait anxiety).

Various explanatory models have been proposed to account for the aforementioned interaction between anxiety and the aging processes. Of note, together the neurotoxicity hypothesis, the vulnerability hypothesis, and reduced rate of neurogenesis shed light on processes contributing to the development and maintenance of trait anxiety and increased frequency of anxious states in older adults (Lupien, King, Meaney and McEwen, 2000). Specifically, concerning aging and anxiety, the vulnerability hypothesis stresses that some of later life anxiety (i.e., state and trait) is resultant from genetic predisposition, exposure to stress during critical developmental periods (i.e., prenatal, early childhood, and adolescence), and distressing life circumstances in adulthood, while the neurotoxicity hypothesis emphasizes increased cell death from chronic activation of the HPA axis. These postulations about the interaction of aging and anxiety are in line with current treatment conceptualizations of anxiety and other mood disorders—specifically, the triple vulnerability theory, which notes a tri-partite contribution (i.e., genetics, early life experiences, and specific psychological factors) to the development of emotional regulation difficulty (Barlow, 2004; Barlow et al., 2010).

Put simply, late life trait and state anxiety are likely a consequence of all or a combination of the following: 1) genetic predisposition to react to stressful life events more aversely, 2) adverse early life experiences, 3) distressing life circumstances in adulthood, 4) neuronal cell death that results from chronic activation of the stress response, and 5) a rate decline of the birth of new neurons that help regulate responses to threating life events. The next section explores the specifics of trait and state anxiety on both neuroanatomical and neuroendocrine levels in more detail.

Neuroanatomical and Neuroendocrine Correlates of State Anxiety

As explored previously, state anxiety refers to a condition of feeling fearful, tense, apprehensive, nervous, and worried, which is frequently associated with physiological arousal. On the most rudimentary level, the amygdala has been linked to "fear learning," allowing for quick responses to threatening stimuli (i.e., connections from the sensory thalamus to the amygdala) such as rapid fear when seeing a twig that resembles a snake (Charney, 2003).

On a neuroendocrine level, threatening situations typically activate the hypothalamic-pituitary-adrenal (HPA) axis, involving a number of hormonal, neuronal, and sensory inputs that form connections with inhibitory (i.e., calming) neurons to manage excitability within this system (Scrable et al., 2009). During HPA axis activation, corticotropin releasing hormone is discharged by hypothalamus (i.e., the "H" in HPA), stimulating the secretion of adrenocorticotropin hormone from the pituitary gland (i.e., the "P" in HPA), which activates the adrenal glands (i.e., the "A" in HPA) to synthesize and secrete stress hormones (i.e., glucocorticoids), such as cortisol and also epinephrine and norepinephrine (Scrable et al., 2009). The result of this activation leads to increased heart rate, muscle strength, blood pressure, and sugar metabolism, which aim to prepare the organism with enough energy to face the threat making the organism becomes more alert, vigilant, and physiologically posed to respond (i.e., increased blood flow to major muscle groups). After the threatening or stressful event, several inhibitory (i.e., calming) neuroendocrine (e.g., adrenal), subcortical (e.g., hypothalamus, hippocampus) and cortical (e.g., frontal cortex) modulating systems aim to return the state of anxiety to a homeostatic state. Over activation of this system, however, has a potentially negative effect on the brain.

To illustrate, consider a racecar that has a reserve of a boost-fuel designed to be utilized sparingly at critical points of races; logically, overuse of this boost-fuel raises the temperature of the engine components, insidiously damages some of parts, and taxes various cooling mechanisms that were designed for intermittent use only. Similarly, over activation of the HPA axis leads to an excess presence of hormones that were designed to be secreted sparingly (i.e., glucocorticoids), which potentially have long-lasting effects on the functioning of the brain regions that regulate their release, likely contributing to the formation of trait anxiety described in the following section (Lupien, McEwen, Gunnar and Heim, 2009).

Neuroanatomical and Neuroendocrine Correlates of Trait Anxiety

Trait anxiety generally relates to a propensity to perceive situations as threatening or aversive, regularly activating the aforementioned anxious states (Wetherell, Reynolds, Gatz and Pedersen, 2002). In addition to playing a role in rapid responses to threatening stimuli, the amygdala is related to more prolonged and propensity for anxious states (i.e., trait anxiety) via connections to neocortical brain regions, producing tendencies such as expectation of criticism while interacting with an authority figure. As such, higher-order (i.e., complex) learning, processing, and maintenance of trait anxiety rely heavily on the plasticity (i.e., flexibility) and integrity of neural network between the amygdala its connections to cortical brain structures that process more complex information.

For example, several areas of the orbital prefrontal cortex share bi-directional connections with the amygdala that play an important role in more sophisticated processing of threatening stimuli and assist in modifying behavior based on punishment, rewards, impact on social surroundings; damage to these connections reduces an individual's ability to adjust to the consequences of positive and negative outcomes (Baxter, Parker, Lindner, Izquierdo and Murray, 2000). Similarly, bi-directional connections between the amygdala and the medial prefrontal cortex have been implicated in weakening learned fear responses, with lesions studies demonstrating abnormal physiological reactions to emotionally provocative stimuli and a reduction in ability to process information regarding a reduced likelihood of aversive social consequences (Damasio, Tranel and Damasio, 1990).

Put simply, a disruption of pathways between the amygdala and the aforementioned select examples of cortical brain structures (i.e., orbital prefrontal cortex and medial prefrontal cortex) appear to lead to abnormal physiological arousal (i.e., HPA axis activation) and continued fear related to aversive consequences (e.g., public criticism, punishment) despite being provided evidence that such consequences are unlikely and improbable; thus, once such an individual deems something as dangerous due to a past experience (i.e., being hit by a car or being criticized at a social gathering), threat is detected and responded to indiscriminately across all environments that even minimally resemble the initial situation even though the evidence suggests otherwise, which resembles characteristics of trait anxiety.

On the neuroendocrine level, studies have demonstrated a negative impact of chronic and repeated activation of the HPA axis throughout the lifespan, leading to vulnerability to acquire trait anxiety due to comprised functioning of the brain region undergoing the most change (Lupien et al., 2000). Namely, as humans age, the brain matures and changes and chronic HPA axis activation adversely impacts these sensitive areas.

First, maternal psychological distress during pregnancy adversely impacts the programming of her offspring's HPA axis modulating or "calming" systems (i.e., hippocampus, frontal cortex and the amygdala), which can lead to an increased likelihood for later-life mood and anxiety disorders (Gutteling, de Weerth and Buitelaar, 2005; Lyons-Ruth, Wolfe and Lyubchik, 2000; O'Connor et al., 2005). Similarly, childhood exposure to chronic or repeated stress (e.g., abuse, maternal depression) significantly impacts the offspring's developing hippocampus and amygdala, leading to increased likelihood for later-life mood disorders and abnormal HPA axis activity (Fries, Hesse, Hellhammer and Hellhammer, 2005; Halligan, Herbert, Goodyer and Murray, 2007; McGowan et al., 2009). Adolescent exposure to chronic or repeated stress (i.e., HPA axis activation) impacts the development of the frontal cortex, which—among other functions—is crucial for regulating one's emotional states; it is unsurprising that research has found that stressful life events during adolescence period frequently precede the onset of anxiety disorders (Lupien et al., 2000; Vouimba, Yaniv and Richter-Levin, 2007).

In adulthood to old age, chronic or repeated activation of the HPA axis primarily impacts hippocampal brain regions (i.e., memory center), with less impact on the frontal cortex and amygdala (Lupien et al., 1998). At this stage, low self-esteem is associated with increased HPA activation and reduced hippocampal volume (Pruessner et al., 2005), presence of depression has been documented to have elevated glucocorticoid levels and decreased hippocampal size (Burke, Davis, Otte and Mohr, 2005; Videbech & Ravnkilde, 2004), and posttraumatic stress disorder has been linked to lower levels of glucocorticoids and reduced hippocampal volume (Smith, 2005; Yehuda, Golier and Kaufman, 2005). It is important to note that the psychopathology leading to these brain changes could represent markers of compromised HPA axis functioning and vulnerability to a disorder due to the aforementioned genetic, prenatal, and developmental factors before adulthood (Lupien et al., 2000).

Neuroanatomical and Neuroendocrine Changes in the Aging Brain

Although a number of psychological and disease factors may play a role in the development and maintenance of anxiety states in the aging brain (e.g., recognition of cognitive and physical decline) (Sinoff & Werner, 2003), expected changes in the nervous system may independently account for some of the prevalence of anxiety in older adults. For example, compared to younger adults, healthy older adults have higher glucocorticoid levels (i.e., stress hormones), which are correlated with decreased hippocampal volume and memory during the aging process (Lupien et al., 1998). Additionally, high glucocorticoid levels during aging appear to have negative effects on prefrontal cortical neuronal functioning, adversely impacting planning, organization, decision making, and more importantly, emotional regulation (Dai, Buijs and Swaab, 2004). Moreover, individuals with high levels of both reported anxiety and clinically significant levels of amyloid-β burden (i.e., peptides involved in Alzheimer's disease) predicted cognitive decline more than anxiety or levels amyloid-β alone (Pietrzak et al., 2015). Of particular relevance is deterioration of neurogenesis (i.e., birth of new neurons) in neural networks of the HPA axis during aging (Scrable et al., 2009).

Even though the birth of new neurons (i.e., neurogenesis) was previously believed to not occur in the adult brain, more recent advances in brain research suggest that neurogenesis persists throughout adulthood in several areas of the brain (Cayre, Malaterre, Scotto-Lomassese, Strambi and Strambi, 2002), including structures responsible for optimal functioning of the HPA axis functioning; however, the rate of neurogenesis in these areas significantly declines as an organism ages (Scrable et al., 2009). Neurogenesis (i.e., birth of new neurons) in the HPA axis generates cells that are inhibitory (i.e., calming), but as one ages, these cells are no longer produced at the same rate relative to younger adults. Thus, this decline in the quantity of neurons dedicated to reducing the excitability of the HPA axis leads to a lowered anxiety threshold (i.e., increased ease of activation of anxious states) and more prolonged instances of physiological arousal associated with HPA activation (i.e., increased heart rate, blood pressure, sugar metabolism) (Scrable et al., 2009). In other words, with a reduced number of neuronal cells that control this stress response, the brain has to extend more effort in returning the HPA axis to a homeostatic state. Consequently, as reviewed previously, excess presence of stress hormones in the blood stream has neurotoxic effects contributing to continued neuronal cell death and brain atrophy (i.e., brain shrinkage) (Scrable et al., 2009).

To review, consider the analogy of a racecar where susceptibility to injury from boost-fuel overuse can be conceptualized on the following levels: design, manufacturing, frequency of boost-fuel use, and decreased availability of replacement parts. First, if the racecar is designed in a manner that is less able to withstand overuse of the boost-fuel (e.g., poor cooling systems, the use of a sensitive metal alloy), reduced optimal functioning of the machine is likely from the get-go. With regard to anxiety, design can be related to genetics, as genetic epidemiological studies have indicated heritability estimates of about 30–50% (Shimada-Sugimoto, Otowa and Hettema, 2015), which is related to an increased propensity for anxious states and traits. Next, if manufacturing errors are made during the racecar's production (e.g., improper forging of the engine metal, faulty boost-fuel switch, damage to the cooling system), the racecar's performance declines and susceptibility to adverse effects of repeated boost-fuel is probable. This relates to various developmentally critical periods, including prenatal, early life experiences, and adolescence with each period being sensitive to excess presence of stress hormones in the area of the brain that is undergoing the most growth. Now, even if the design of the racecar is adequate and no manufacturing errors were made, overuse of the boost-fuel will inevitably lead to reduced performance, as the racecar boost-fuel was designed for intermittent use only. Similarly, in the absence of a genetic predisposition or adverse events during critical developmental periods, individuals will likely experience dysregulation of the HPA axis if exposed to prolonged or extreme stressors, such as war or violence. As the racecar ages, the reduced availability of replacement parts becomes problematic, and without these replacement parts, the racecar is forced to compromise with what is available and endures a more rapid decline in performance due to overheating. Similarly, as humans age, a reduced production of new "calming" neurons decrease the efficiency of the brain to manage the stress response, which further exacerbates the damage to brain cells (i.e., neurotoxicity) resulting in prolonged anxious states and eventually trait anxiety. While this deterioration may appear to have inevitable negative effects on emotional regulation, neuroimaging techniques have also revealed positive plasticity in the brain, with compensatory recruitment of areas involved in planning and problem solving (i.e., prefrontal brain regions) and reorganization of brain areas (i.e., altered lateralization) to adjust to life's demands, especially in the older adults who have made significant intellectual, social, and physical investments leading to neural reserves utilized later in life (Reuter-Lorenz & Park, 2010). Thus, if the racecar has made significant investments in spare parts and upgraded to more durable main components, the effects of boost-fuel is less detrimental than racecars that have made less of an investment in these components.

Defining Cognitive Functioning

Prior to specifically examining the effects of aging, age-related conditions, and their impact on cognitive function, we first define cognitive functioning and corresponding neurodegenerative disorders. For the purpose of this chapter, we will be looking at cognitive functioning as an overarching term for several different abilities of the human brain, including memory, learning, processing speed, problem solving, visuospatial skills, language abilities, and executive functioning. This also includes neural substrates related to emotion.

Cognition on a Continuum: Age and Age-Related Conditions

It is commonly known that there is a relative decline in cognitive and physical functioning in the aging population. These changes are associated with overall changes in the structure of the brain (Park & Reuter-Lorenz, 2009), as well as the molecular and chemical alterations. Most notably, the cortical thickness decreases and subsequently, specific areas of the brain, including the hippocampus (important to learning and memory), are prone to shrinkage (Xu et al., 2008).

Age-related cognitive decline is a well-known phenomenon, with increasing incidence after age 85 ("2014 Alzheimer's disease facts and figures," 2014; Tom et al., 2015). Normal aging has been associated with a decrease in brain volume, with corresponding increase in ventricular volume (Liu et al., 2003; Orellana et al., 2016; Scahill et al., 2003). More specifically, the largest changes are noted in the hippocampus, anterior dorsal frontal lobe, and select subcortical structures (e.g., thalamus, basal ganglia) (Beauchet, Launay, Annweiler and Allali, 2015; Liu et al., 2003; Scahill et al., 2003; Xu et al., 2008). Reductions in hippocampal volumes are more prominent in those with MCI when compared to non-MCI individuals (Beauchet et al., 2015). Lateral frontal and parietal regions are also vulnerable to the effects of aging (Kakimoto et al., 2015). Imaging studies have also found associations between increasing age and reduced volumes of the intracranial cavity, total brain volume, gray matter volume, and total cerebellar volume (Liu et al., 2003). Additionally, cortical white matter is prone to shrinkage and plaques and neurofibrillary tangles accrue, resulting in neuronal loss (Guttmann et al., 1998). Temporal and prefrontal lobes are also noted to exhibit reduced metabolic activity (Xu et al., 2008). Collectively, this suggests that in general, a pattern of loss within the aging brain seems to proceed from anterior to posterior regions at a gradual and progressive rate (Kravitz, Kim, Faust-Socher, Rogers and Miller, 2008).

Age-Related Conditions

Although most abilities decline with age, certain pathologies lead to a more precipitous decline. The following section provides a brief summary on several of the most common neurodegenerative disorders that specifically affect the aging population.

Mild Cognitive Impairment

Individuals with mild cognitive impairment (MCI) demonstrate cognitive declines that are in excess of normal aging (Cullum & Liff, 2014). However, these declines are not yet sufficient for a diagnosis of dementia. In the initial stages, the signs and symptoms may be subtle and progress in a gradual nature. As such, MCI can impact one or several areas of functioning, in which subclassifications of single- or multiple domain MCI are warranted. However, 70% of those diagnosed with MCI will eventually progress to dementia as the neurodegenerative process continues, for some taking up to 15-to-20 years for full conversion (Rizzi, Rosset and Roriz-Cruz, 2014). There are several types of MCI, in which subtypes are dependent upon the number of cognitive domains affected and whether there are deficits in memory (Petersen, 2007). It is noted that MCI amnestic type is the most common presentation and is likely to exhibit impairments in either verbal or visual memory (Cullum & Liff, 2014; Petersen et al., 1997). It is important to note that MCI does not dramatically interfere with activities of daily living and is commonly expressed as a subtle change from premorbid functioning (Cullum & Liff, 2014). Research suggests that age, gender, race, occupational and educational achievements, and medical conditions can increase the risk for developing of MCI (Kravitz et al., 2008; Miller et al., 2012). For detailed information about MCI, please see our previous book chapter (Kravitz et al., 2008) and publications by Petersen (Petersen, 2006, 2007; Petersen et al., 2001; Petersen & O'Brien, 2006; Petersen et al., 1997).

Dementia

Dementia is attributed to the development of impairments of memory or related cognitive functioning in the aging brain (Cummings & Benson, 1992; Whalley, 2015). Dementia is a progressive disease affecting over 20 million individuals worldwide, having increased incidence with advanced age (Ferri et al., 2005; Tom et al., 2015). Collectively, these impairments subsequently impact the person's ability to independently function in social, occupational, or familial settings, as well as impacting functions of daily living (Liepelt-Scarfone et al., 2013).

Importantly, dementia is known as a global impairment, and as such, much affect multiple areas of cognitive functioning (Gurland, Dean, Copeland, Gurland and Golden, 1982; Whalley, 2015). It is a global condition, and not necessarily affiliated with on single type of cognitive deficit (Cummings, Benson and Levine, 1984; Deptula, Singh and Pomara, 1993). However, it is common in which one cognitive deficit, mainly memory, will predominate, with a progression of global impairments as the disease continues (Cummings et al., 1984). Dementia typically occurs in the sixth-to-seventh decade of life, with occurrences as early as the fifth decade and can be diagnosed up until death (Deptula et al., 1993; Whalley, 2015).

As a part of the neurodegenerative process, dementia accounts for the majority of disorders amongst older adults. Recent research estimates that the prevalence of dementia increases by age range: 2-3% among those aged 70-75, and 20-25% of those aged 85 or older (Ferri et al., 2005; Kukull et al., 2002; Rizzi et al., 2014; Tom et al., 2015). Additionally, gender affects prevalence, as recent studies have found that females are more likely susceptible to the disease (Ferri et al., 2005; Rizzi et al., 2014). Life expectancy is also found to decrease with a higher age at diagnosis (Tom et al., 2015).

From a life course perspective, other factors, including environmental and social considerations, greatly influence the clinical diagnosis of dementia. As such, the severity of the illness is viewed on a continuum, including mild cognitive impairment, which precludes dementia, and other neurodegenerative diseases that occur as progressive variants of dementia.

What we refer to as Alzheimer's disease (AD) is the most frequently occurring form of late-onset dementia and has a reported prevalence of 5% amongst adults over the age of 65, with the prevalence rate doubling every five years (Cullum & Liff, 2014). Once diagnosed, most people experience a gradual decline from onset to death over a period of eight to ten years (Cullum & Liff, 2014; Whalley, 2015). Most commonly, the disease follows a temporal-to-frontal spread (i.e., impacting memory/language and then executive skills) and eventually involves the majority of systems in the brain (Cullum & Liff, 2014).

Following AD, frontotemporal dementias (FTD) are the second most common variant of dementia (Whalley, 2015). While the global prevalence of dementia is estimated to be 5-7% for individuals over the age of 60 (Prince et al., 2013), frontotemporal dementia accounts for 10% of all patients with dementing diseases or 0.5-0.7% of adults over the age of 60 (Mendez & Perryman, 2002). For patients with an onset prior to age 65, frontotemporal dementia accounts for 20-50% of all early onset neurodegenerative dementias (Mendez, Lauterbach and Sampson, 2008). FTD is characterized by behavioral, language, and/or motor impairment that precede other deficits (Bush, 2014). Another variant of dementia is vascular dementia (VaD), which accounts for 1.2 to 4.2% of people over 65 years old, with age of onset between 60 and 75 years (Hebert & Brayne, 1995). Symptoms most commonly reported include deficits in executive functioning, slower processing speed, and deficits in attention (Swihart, 2014). However, Vascular dementia is most notably evident with select and patchy declines among several cognitive domains.

IMPACT ON COGNITIVE FUNCTIONING

To understand age-related conditions and their impact on functioning, it may help to start with a quick review of the cognitive changes that accompany normal aging. As with most pathologies, normal aging is not a homogeneous concept with significant variability between individuals of the same age (Salthouse, 2009); however, there are several cognitive areas that generally undergo age-related decline in a healthy individual throughout the lifespan (Shineman et al., 2010). Specifically, memory, reasoning ability, spatial visualization, and processing speed begin declining after the age of 20, while vocabulary, comprehension, and general fund of knowledge increase until approximately age 50-60 and then decline mildly (Salthouse, 2009). As an individual ages, increased forgetfulness is more commonly noticed, with up to 41% of healthy individuals aged 50-59 and approximately 52% of healthy individuals aged 60-69 noticing some memory decline (Small, La Rue, Komo, Kaplan and Mandelkern, 1995). It is of important to note that even on a neuroanatomical level, the dynamic structural changes that occur in the normal aging brain are often times clinically difficult to differentiate from the initial stage of neurodegenerative processes, such as Alzheimer's disease (Small et al., 1994; Thompson et al., 1998).

Cognitive Impairments Relative to Age-Related Conditions in Older Adults

A common complaint among older adults is a decline in memory. Age-related memory impairments affect over 40% of older adults and are characterized by subjective memory complaints and a decline in objective memory performances (Caselli et al., 2009; Salthouse, 2009). The most significant declines are observed in working memory, recent long-term memories, encoding and retrieval, and prospective memories (Braaten, Parsons, McCue, Sellers and Burns, 2006; Small, 2001). In older adults, we also see changes in language, with a decrease in fluency relative to intact confrontation naming. Processing speed is also affected and is noted by a slowing of reaction time and an overall slowing of processing incoming information (Braaten et al., 2006; Salthouse, 1996). By contrast, immediate and simple attention for auditory information remains preserved (Salthouse & Babcock, 1991). The aging brain is also characterized by a widespread decline in executive functioning abilities. Older adults are observed to perform poorly on tasks of inhibition, cognitive flexibility, adaptability, and problem solving (Greenwood, 2000; Salthouse, Atkinson and Berish, 2003), forms of abstract reasoning and simple non-verbal problem solving abilities remain intact (Rogers, Kang and Miller, 2007; Salthouse et al., 2003).

All of these deficits become significantly pronounced as the development of cognitive impairment progresses. For example, symptoms in Alzheimer's disease are typically marked by a pervasive deficit in memory acquisition and storage (Cullum & Liff, 2014). Additional impairments are noted in the domains of episodic memory, executive functioning, perceptual speed, as well as global cognitive ability (Backman, Jones, Berger, Laukka and Small, 2005; Backman & Small, 2007; Persson, Wallin, Levander and Minthon, 2009). Conversely, cases of Frontotemporal dementia are more commonly noted by initial changes in personality, interpersonal conduct, and emotional regulation (Bush, 2014). Specific changes often include: social withdrawal, poor decision-making, impulsivity, apathy, inertia, reduced motivation, and decreased empathy (Bush, 2014). While the nature of the cognitive profile affiliated with Vascular Dementia is highly variable, patients tend to display frontal deficits (e.g., impulsivity, disorganization), with select and patchy declines in other domains (Braaten et al., 2006).

Resilience and Cognitive Reserve

Despite all the evidence suggesting structural, as well as functional loss in older adults, a discussion of resilience in this particular population is warranted. Within the field of aging and memory, a nuanced term known as "cognitive reserve" is an important concept that is gaining widespread attention.

The concept of "cognitive reserve" describes the ability of the aging brain to use its available resources in order to better tolerate age-related changes and disease-related pathologies in regard to symptom presentation (Stern, 2012). Early research suggested that being exposed to an enriched environment during early life may serve as a protective agent against the cognitive deficits associated with aging (Satz, 1993). However, current research has narrowed this belief to be more specifically related to educational and occupational exposure, as it relates to increasing cognitive reserve. For example, studies have indicated that when comparing participants with low or high levels of cognitive reserve (as measured by educational and occupational attainment), those with low cognitive reserve had to apply greater effort in order to achieve the same level of cognitive performance as those with high cognitive reserve on a memory task (Lopez et al., 2014). Further, neuroimaging has been used to study this phenomenon, and has suggested that in preclinical Alzheimer's disease patients, higher education serves as a compensatory mechanism to maintain cognitive ability, as shown by a decrease in FDG-PET metabolism (Ewers, Insel, Stern and Weiner, 2013), and higher cognitive reserve has even been associated with a decrease in age-related alterations in cerebrospinal biomarkers of Alzheimer's disease (Almeida et al., 2015).

In regard to treatment options, the Tasmanian Healthy Brain Project, conducted in Australia, indicated that older adults, aged 50-79, who engaged in further education (part-time university study) displayed an increase in cognitive reserve over a 4-year period, suggesting that it is never too late to build cognitive reserve (Lenehan et al., 2015).

EFFECTS OF ANXIETY ON COGNITIVE FUNCTIONING

As previously discussed, functional as well as structural changes occur in the aging brain. While these changes are characteristic of normal aging, we have learned that emotional stress and corresponding disorders can negatively correlate with cognitive functioning. Chronic mood symptoms and disorders, such as anxiety, can have deleterious effects on cognition, especially with regard to learning and memory (Joels, Pu, Wiegert, Oitzl and Krugers, 2006; McEwen & Sapolsky, 1995). While several of these psychiatric symptoms may be secondary to the effects of neurodegenerative disease, it is important to recognize that even mild emotional difficulties can exacerbate cognitive and functional decline (Mantella et al., 2007; Mather, 2012). In this section, we will review the literature in regard to the effects of anxiety upon cognitive functioning; however, it is important to note that numerous factors can contribute to the level of functioning in the aging brain. As such, we will report how anxiety effects cognitive functioning as a separate construct within the paradigm of neurodegenerative disorders. Understanding these effects and processes is crucial to guiding those within the geriatric population toward positive adaptations, which we will discuss later.

Current research highlights anxiety's impact upon cognitive functioning in older adults; specifically highlighting deficits in attention, reading, mathematics, reasoning, and memory (Edwards, Moore, Champion and Edwards, 2015). More specifically, anxiety has been found to impair processing efficiency, cause adverse effects on task performance, negatively impact attentional control, impair efficiency (and often effectiveness), as well as negatively impact a person's ability to complete and finish select tasks (Berggren & Derakshan, 2013; Eysenck, Derakshan, Santos and Calvo, 2007). Whether the anxiety is treated as a unitary construct (Barisa, 2014; Scrable et al., 2009), or examined as state versus trait anxiety, research suggests that interventions (e.g., psychotropic medications; leisurely activities; psychotherapy) can be useful in treating the symptoms.

State Anxiety

State anxiety (i.e., transient feelings of tension, apprehension, nervousness, and worry) has been documented to impact cognitive functioning, specifically in regard to the working memory processing and storage system, which is comprised of a phonological loop (i.e., temporary storage and manipulation of verbal information), the visuospatial sketchpad (i.e., temporary storage and manipulation of visual images), and the central executive system (i.e., maintains attention and coordinates other subsystems) (Wetherell et al., 2002). Working memory has a limited capacity, and as its resources are taxed due to increased interference (i.e., anxious states of worry and self-preoccupation) a decline in performance is observed. Compared to younger adults, older adults, regardless of presence of anxiety, display declines in the processing speed aspect of working memory and less so in the storage aspect of working memory (Salthouse & Babcock, 1991). However, older adults are more susceptible to the effects of anxiety (i.e., specifically in verbal working memory tasks involving the phonological loop and the central executive) with research documenting an additive effect of poorer performance in processing verbal information and complex visuospatial tasks that require the involvement of the central executive system (Wetherell et al., 2002) and reduced performance on delayed verbal memory, executive functions, and information processing speed compared to controls (Booth et al., 2006). A notable impact on learning and memory has also been documented (Beaudreau & O'Hara, 2008).

Trait Anxiety

Trait anxiety (i.e., propensity for anxious states) has been associated with inefficient processing abilities, namely those who are more anxious in nature tend to frequently perceive threats in specific encountered situations (Yiend, 2010). Additionally, trait-based anxiety presents with poorer cognitive performance on tasks that measure response inhibition, emotional regulation, attentional shift, and visual tracking (Bar-Haim, Kerem, Lamy and Zakay, 2010; Berggren & Derakshan, 2013; Mathews, Fox, Yiend and Calder, 2003). Additionally, compared to state anxiety, trait anxiety has been negatively correlated to creative performance for both visual and verbal tasks, as cognitive resources (i.e., working memory, memory retrieval, and attention) are devoted more to modulating the anxiety and threat detection than to fully engaging in a creative task (Byron & Khazanchi, 2011). More specifically, this significantly restricts the ability to consider alternatives, generate mental images, make novel connections, and sustain attention (Byron & Khazanchi, 2011). As a whole, trait anxiety appears to be related to poorer performance resulting from distraction, especially when presented with visual distracting stimuli (McTeague, Shumen, Wieser, Lang and Keil, 2011).

Quantitatively, research has found that trait anxiety directly affects the executive control network (i.e., the ability to control our own behavior/emotions in order to achieve intended goal), while state anxiety is noted to be associated with an over-functioning of the alerting (e.g., achieving and maintaining a general state of activation of cognitive functions) and orienting (e.g., attentional focus to particular stimuli) networks (Martella, Casagrande and Lupianez, 2011; Pacheco-Unguetti, Acosta, Callejas and Lupianez, 2010). For example, with older adults, both state and trait anxiety has been associated with significantly poorer performance on verbal abstraction, analogies, and practical problem-solving tests (Cohen, Eisdorfer, Vitaliano and Bloom, 1980; LaRue & D'Elia, 1985) and poorer verbal learning in late life (Deptula et al., 1993). In addition to finding poorer episodic memory in older adults with Generalized Anxiety Disorder relative to psychiatric controls, significant difficulty during set shifting has also been documented (Mantella et al., 2007). Overall, research suggests that anxiety in older adults appears to compromise verbal learning and memory, central executive functions, working memory, and emotional regulation (Wetherell et al., 2002).

Differentiating the Impact of Anxiety and How It Relates to Overall Functioning

Generalizing from the studies reviewed above to everyday functioning is a difficult task, given that most of the research was conducted under rigorous experimental conditions; however, several inferences can be made. For instance, given that state anxiety (i.e., transient feelings of tension, apprehension, nervousness, and worry) impacts working memory capacity and learning, older adults reporting high levels of state anxiety will likely struggle in retaining and learning complex (particularly if it is verbal) information, completing several tasks at once, and rapid processing of information. As trait anxiety (i.e., propensity for anxious states) predisposes older adults to distractibility and poor response inhibition, they may have difficulties during everyday aspects of life that include new approaches to solving a problem and sustaining attention on tasks that require full concentration. Again, given the significant interaction between state and trait anxiety, the presence of both trait and state anxiety may result in increased difficulty for: understanding abstract ideas, learning new information and novel ways of solving problems, and handling more than one task, or activity, at the same time (Norton et al., 2012; Tinetti, Inouye, Gill and Doucette, 1995).

Apart from psychological distress and its impact on cognitive tasks, researchers have documented functional impacts of anxiety across other domains in later stages of life. For instance, in a sample of community dwelling older adults aged 65 and above, repeated measures of anxiety and activity limitations (i.e., social restriction, mobility, and limitations in instrumental activities of daily living) demonstrated that both trait anxiety and the presence of an anxiety disorder (i.e., met diagnostic criteria) were associated with poorer functioning (Norton et al., 2012). Specifically, trait anxiety was associated with social restriction while the presence of an anxiety disorder was related to more profound limitations in instrumental activities of daily living (IADL), such as driving, managing finances, etc. For women with GAD, anxiety was a significant predictor that they would have more difficulty with IADLs over the next three years (Brenes et al., 2005). In a study (age 72 and older), anxiety symptoms resulted in limitations of basic activities of daily living (ADL), such as grooming, cleaning, etc., even after controlling for physical functioning (Tinetti et al., 1995).

METHODS FOR TREATING ANXIETY AS IT RELATES TO COGNITIVE TRAINING AND HEALTH

Research has shown that the brain's neuroplasticity enables it to change with certain experiences and engagements (Green & Bavelier, 2008). Although the brain's ability to adapt and utilize cognitive reserve decreases with age, research suggests that individuals can improve their overall brain functioning and emotional wellbeing by engaging in various activities that will be discussed in the following section. As noted previously, reducing anxiety symptoms can positively impact the brain's structural and functional abilities. Anxiety can be mediated by a variety of exercises, including: meditation, relaxing/coping exercises, psychotherapy, and psychotropic medications. Additionally, maintaining healthy nutrition and remaining physically, mentally, and socially active can contribute to the brain's neuroplasticity and preservation of functioning. Here, we review the literature from recent research related to these topics.

Psychotherapy

Psychotherapy is the most common avenue of treatment for anxiety (Mohlman, 2013), and recent research has suggested that psychotherapy is the most effective treatment at alleviating symptoms within the older adults population and can be useful in addressing subsequent cognitive declines associated with anxiety. Inadequate coping skills can be addressed in psychotherapy, thus decreasing additional risk for anxiety (Vink et al., 2008). Psychotherapy has often been selected over pharmacological and combined treatments, with the most preferred treatments being: Cognitive-Behavioral Therapy (CBT), stress management, and supportive therapy (Mohlman, 2013).

Among recent research, CBT was noted as the most favorable treatment with the most effective outcomes. One randomized trial on older adults with generalized anxiety disorder (GAD) found that the intervention group receiving CBT significantly improved in their symptom presentations, as measured by a number of anxiety scales, over a period of six months (Stanley et al., 2014). Additionally, findings indicated that those receiving one year of CBT treatment were not only found to have a reduction in symptoms when formally assessed, but self-reported a lessening of symptoms and an increased quality of life (Barrowclough et al., 2001). Moreover, the CBT group maintained improvement and had a significantly higher response to treatment compared to those in the control group (Barrowclough et al., 2001).

Recent research has also supported the efficacy of brief CBT options for those with state-based anxiety. Results indicated that brief treatment of late-life generalized anxiety disorder is beneficial and found greater improvements than those in the discussion group-therapy control (Wetherell et al., 2003). Most recently research has focused on the popular treatment known as Acceptance and Commitment Therapy (ACT). Preliminary findings have suggested that the geriatric population is well suited for treating GAD (Wetherell et al., 2011). Both symptoms of worry and depression were noted to improve and similar reductions were reported when compared to those in the CBT group, concluding that ACT may have similar results to CBT (Wetherell et al., 2011). Moreover, it is important to note that research supports and emphasizes the importance of clinical fit in which the client feels supported and comfortable within the selected therapeutic modality (Craske et al., 2009).

Psychotropic/Medical Interventions

People with anxiety often turn to primary care physicians in seeking treatment (Bystritsky, Khalsa, Cameron and Schiffman, 2013). Due to the involvement of the neurotransmitter system in the pathophysiology of anxiety, pharmacological treatments are often the first line of treatment as they intervene at the biological level (Bystritsky et al., 2013; Mitte, Noack, Steil and Hautzinger, 2005; Mokhber, Azarpazhooh, Khajehdaluee, Velayati and Hopwood, 2010). A meta-analysis on anxiety disorders in older adults found that pharmacotherapy was more effective at reducing anxiety symptoms when compared with behavioral interventions alone (Pinquart & Duberstein, 2007). Common classes of drugs known to act on these neurotransmitter pathways in the treatment of anxiety include the following: selective serotonin reuptake inhibitors (SSRIs), serotonin-norepinephrine reuptake inhibitors (SNRIs), benzodiazepines, antiepileptic medications, and tricyclic antidepressants, among additional medications, with SSRIs being a first-line drug (Bandelow et al., 2008; Bystritsky et al., 2013; Farach et al., 2012; Mokhber et al., 2010). Benzodiazepines have been shown to be effective in reducing depressive symptoms among patients with GAD, as measured by subjective rating scales such as Hamilton Rating Scale for Depression (Mitte et al., 2005). Because of this, benzodiazepines are also commonly prescribed in the treatment of anxiety, with between 9.5% and 20% of older adults in community-dwelling populations receiving this treatment option (Cook, Biyanova, Masci and Coyne, 2007; Lindsey, 2009; Llorente, David, Golden and Silverman, 2000). Sertraline and buspirone have also been found to have significant anxiolytic properties among older adults, as measured by subjective scales of anxiety (Mokhber et al., 2010).

Among the side effects of certain psychotropic therapies (Bandelow et al., 2008), cognitive changes may also occur. One study on older individuals found psychotropic drug use to be associated with lower cognitive scores (Paterniti, Dufouil, Bisserbe and Alperovitch, 1999). Specifically, chronic users of benzodiazepine were more at risk for declines in the areas of executive functioning, including attention. While benzodiazepine use has been associated with cognitive declines in a number of domains in older adults, other anxiolytics, such as buspirone, show similar effects, but to a lesser degree (Chamberlain et al., 2007). Despite the potential for side effects, anxiolytics have been shown to effectively reduce symptoms in older adults, including symptoms of depression. In fact, when compared to middle-aged adults, older adults are 7 to 18 times more likely to use psychotropic drugs (Voyer & Martin, 2003). Based on this, pharmacologic interventions continue to serve as first-line therapy for anxiety and anxiety-related disorders.

Stress Reduction and Management

As previously mentioned, chronic and situational stress can exacerbate cognitive decline and worsen symptoms of anxiety (Berggren & Derakshan, 2013; Eysenck et al., 2007); as such, two of the leading treatments, mindfulness and leisure, are discussed below. In conjunction with psychotherapy and/or psychotropic medications, stress-reducing practices have been found to lessen symptoms of chronic and situational stress, while improving quality of life in older adults.

Meditative/Mindfulness Practices

There is growing research in support of the anxiety relieving effects of mindfulness techniques. Interventions incorporating mindfulness for older adults have shown reductions in anxiety (Sorrell, 2015). Research has continued to indicate mindfulness as a favorable treatment among older adults and specifically for the treatment of anxiety. When examined at pre- and post-treatment time points, mindfulness participants noted significant improvement for both anxiety and mood symptoms (Hofmann, Sawyer, Witt and Oh, 2010). Additionally, research has found several health benefits of utilizing Mindfulness-based stress reduction (MBSR). Preliminary data suggested that MBSR may help a broad range of individuals to cope with their clinical and nonclinical problems, while simultaneously reducing several health risks, including reductions in high blood pressure (Grossman, Niemann, Schmidt and Walach, 2004).

Furthermore, sleep disturbances are often present in anxious individuals, further exacerbating cognitive difficulties, and are especially prevalent among older adults. In fact, it has been estimated that up to half of older adults have some form of sleep problems (Black, O'Reilly, Olmstead, Breen and Irwin, 2015; Crowley, 2011). One randomized clinical trial assessing mindful awareness practices in older adults (mean age 66) reported significant improvements in sleep habits in the intervention group, as measured by the Pittsburgh Sleep Quality Index (PSQI) (Black et al., 2015). Studies have specifically investigated the effects of meditation, one form of mindfulness, on various cognitive domains. One review of seven studies on older adults and those who have neurodegenerative disease, suggested that the practice of meditation may show gains in the areas of attention, memory, verbal fluency, and cognitive flexibility (Marciniak et al., 2014).

Leisure Activities

As one grows older, it is assumed that there will be more time for leisure activities, which can have a positive impact on both cognition and mood (Leung, Leung and Lam, 2011). Recent studies have shown that a higher level of late-life leisure activity participation is significantly associated with better cognitive function in the older adult populations (Leung et al., 2011). According to Leung and colleagues (2011), late-life activities, particularly intellectual activities, were associated with higher levels of brain functioning, even amongst those with previously diagnosed neurocognitive disorders. Similarly, Tesky and colleagues (2011) found that participation in-group leisure activities resulted in positive effects on cognition. Specifically, results reported an enhanced speed of information processing and an improvement in subjective memory decline (Tesky, Thiel, Banzer and Pantel, 2011). Additionally, research has shown that an influx in leisurely activities is negatively correlated with stress in older adults (Patterson, 1996). Moreover, recent studies have demonstrated a strong influence of satisfaction with leisure activities on quality of life (Leitner & Leitner, 2012). Similarly, results showed that when occupational activities were depleted, elevated levels of anxiety and depression were noted; however, anxious and depressive symptoms were significantly reduced when those activities were augmented (Dunn, Trivedi and O'Neal, 2001). Examples of leisure activities include but are not limited to the following: reading, social engagements, games of skill; support groups; artistic expression (Dunn, Trivedi and O'Neal, 2001; Leung et al., 2011; Tesky et al., 2011). This shows that leisure, whether independently or in a group setting, can be attributed to improvements of cognitive and emotional functioning in older adults and should therefore be utilized in treatment planning for older adults.

Brain Healthy Diet

Research has shown that a brain healthy diet, including moderate caloric intake, high consumption rates of antioxidants and omega-3 fatty acids, as well as reduced sugar and glycemic carbohydrate consumption, can positively impact cognitive functioning (Gutierrez & Isaacson, 2013; Panza et al., 2004; Solfrizzi, Panza and Capurso, 2003). The following discussion reviews several studies examining overall brain healthy nutrition as well a specific dietary supplementation for consideration. Additionally, eating healthy and appropriate dietary supplementation was correlated with a decrease in anxiety and depression (Gautam et al., 2012).

Recent findings have shown dietary effects on cognitive functioning (Solfrizzi et al., 2003). More specifically, increased intake of monounsaturated fatty acids was noted to be associated with a higher level of protection against cognitive decline (Panza et al., 2004; Solfrizzi et al., 2003). Additional research has suggested that specific dietary changes rich in vegetables, fruits, fish, and low consumption of carbohydrates and saturated fat can act as preventative measures in the development of AD in older adults (Gutierrez & Isaacson, 2013). Moreover, diets high in fat increase risk for cognitive decline, while consumption of fish, antioxidants, and olive oils were noted to reduce prevalence of AD (Goodwin, 1983). In addition, antioxidants may be protective against cognitive decline as they can alleviate the oxidative stress produced by free radicals in the brain, which can improve function in the aging brain (Fusco, Colloca, Monaco and Cesari, 2007; Lobo, Patil, Phatak and

Chandra, 2010). Additional evidence has suggested the importance of moderating caloric intake and increasing necessary vitamin (C, B12, E) consumption for cognitive health (Goodwin, 1983; Gutierrez & Isaacson, 2013).

Research has also shown that changes to your diet may make some difference to your general mood or sense of well-being (Murphy & Mercer, 2013). Studies have indicated that, when compared to healthy individuals, those with GAD and depression have significantly lower levels of vitamins A, C, and E, which are nonenzymatic antioxidants (Gautam et al., 2012). After 6 weeks of dietary supplementation, significant increase in blood levels of vitamins A and C were noted, as well as vitamin E in the GAD group only, with significant decrease in anxiety and depression (Gautam et al., 2012). This evidence supports the role for diet in the important connections between psychology, physiology, and behavior (Murphy & Mercer, 2013).

Physical Exercise

Similar to diet, the effects of exercise on cognitive functioning have become an increasingly popular area of research, much of which has examined both the cognitive and emotional enhancements. In regard to cognition, recent studies suggest physical activity is directly associated with improved mood and enhancement of cognitive processing (Hogan, Mata and Carstensen, 2013). Moderate and vigorous exercise activities have also been indicated as a protective factor against strokes and possibly Alzheimer's disease (Weih, Degirmenci, Kreil and Kornhuber, 2010). At a neuroanatomical level, studies have found that participating in weekly aerobic training facilitates significant increases in both gray and white matter brain regions, signifying an improvement in overall brain functioning (Colcombe & Kramer, 2003). Moreover, physical activity has been shown to positively correlate with improvement in cognitive processes, primarily executive control processes (Verstynen et al., 2012).

A review of the literature on the effects of exercise on mood states, including anxiety, indicate that exercising can be associated with a reduction in the presentation of anxiety symptomatology (Byrne & Byrne, 1993). Extended exposure to stress can cause pathological effects on the brain, causing an increase in glucocorticoids, which result in a higher level of hippocampal atrophy (Sapolsky, 1996). Therefore, higher levels of stress, including anxiety, may contribute to cognitive decline. Research has shown support for an increase in brain plasticity through exercise and behavior activation (Cotman & Berchtold, 2002). Exercise also enhances brain plasticity through increased production of brain-derived neurotrophic factor (BDNF) (Young, 1979). Mice studies have shown increased neurogenesis in the hippocampus through running (van Praag, Christie, Sejnowski and Gage, 1999), and another study suggested improvement through exercise in areas of perceptual reasoning, psychomotor speed, and associate learning (Young, 1979). An additional study reported that increased physical activity, when compared to minimal activity, is associated with a moderate reduction of incident AD (Young, 1979). Patients with high levels of anaerobic exercise were noted to benefit from a 41% reduction of future risk for developing AD (Young, 1979). Together, the above studies in addition to those conducted by Weigh et al. (2007, 2009) (Weih et al., 2009; Weih, Wiltfang and Kornhuber, 2007) support psychical activity as a nonpharmocologic prevention for cognitive decline, and/or specific neurocognitive disorders (e.g., AD). As such, if physical activity were performed at a higher rate, the ever-increasing burden and psychological effects of cognitive decline could in fact be amended (Young, 1979). As such, the effects of exercise are proven to enhance both cognitive functioning and emotional wellbeing in the older adult population.

Cognitive Remediation

Because cognitive decline can be a direct result from anxiety, and because some individuals with experience anxiety due to changes in their cognition (or when diagnosed with MCI or dementia), it can beneficial to participate in programs that are specifically designed for the purpose of improving and maintaining cognitive functioning. Structured and standardized programs geared toward teaching specific skills and strategies can be taught one on one, in a classroom setting, or by computer. Many of these programs also address mood symptoms (Spaulding, Reed, Sullivan, Richardson and Weiler, 1999). Cognitive remediation may be addressed through: *cognitive stimulation*, which provides a range of cognitive and social activities to stimulate multiple cognitive domains (Cicerone et al., 2000); *cognitive training* (Miller, Ercoli, Kim and Small, 2010; Sohlberg, 2012), which involves repetition of multiple tasks targeting a specific function (e.g., memory training to improve learning/recall); *cognitive rehabilitation*, which is a more person-centered approach targeting impaired functioning and typically following sudden decline or injury due to stroke, head injury or other causes (Cicerone et al., 2000); or a collective approach which includes several of the above programs (Huntley, Gould, Liu, Smith and Howard, 2015; Sohlberg, 2012).

Cognitive stimulation has been found to improve scores of overall functioning, including performance on the MMSE, and more specifically working memory and attention (Cicerone et al., 2000; Huntley et al., 2015), while cognitive training has been associated with improvements in attention, memory, and language skills (Miller et al., 2010; Sohlberg, 2012). Additionally, cognitive rehabilitation has been associated with improvements for visual working memory, daily functioning, and memory self-efficacy with MCI patients (Barnes et al., 2009; Cicerone et al., 2000), and language and speech production with stroke patients (Cicerone et al., 2000), just to name a few of the many research findings associated with cognitive rehabilitation. Overall, cognitive interventions, including cognitive stimulation, training, and rehabilitation, show immense promise as a method of improving or preserving cognitive functioning in older adults.

CONCLUSION

As this chapter has discussed in detail, anxiety can present itself in up to 20% of older adults (Scrable et al., 2009), and can often be in response to life events that are common to aging, including: social isolation, poor health, financial insecurity, and impending death (Flint, 1994). The nature of this anxiety can be classified as state anxiety, or anxiety that occurs in response to a specific situation, or trait anxiety, which manifests as more of a chronic personality trait. Either way, anxiety can compound many of the problems that one may already be experiencing as they age. Consider again the analogy of the human brain to the racecar: first, genetic predispositions to anxiety (precursors to trait anxiety) are akin to a faulty design for the racecar; second, developmental complications mirror glitches in the manufacturing stage of the parts of the racecar; third, overexposure to anxiety provoking events (state anxiety) can deplete important neurotransmitters needed for healthy brain functioning, as overuse of the boost-fuel will inevitably lead to reduced performance; and lastly, atrophy often seen in the aging brain (akin to the reduced availability of replacement parts for the racecar), lends itself to decreased performance of the brain (and racecar), with a more rapid decline over time. As this analogy so animatedly expresses, anxiety, whether it be trait or state, impacts the brain's functioning at every stage in life, culminating in the aggregate impacts in late life.

Further, it is commonly known that there is a relative decline in cognitive and physical functioning in the aging population, which is associated with structural, molecular, and chemical changes in the brain (Park & Reuter-Lorenz, 2009), with the largest changes documented in the hippocampus, anterior dorsal frontal lobe, and select subcortical structures (e.g., thalamus, basal ganglia) (Beauchet et al., 2015; Liu et al., 2003; Scahill et al., 2003; Xu et al., 2008). Naturally, as these changes occur, it is common for aging individuals to experience some declines in cognitive functioning, namely in memory, reasoning ability, spatial visualization, and processing speed; however, some individuals experience a more significant impact, in excess of normal aging, lending themselves to cognitively associated age-related conditions such as Mild Cognitive Impairment, Dementia, and Alzheimer's disease, to name the most common.

This being said, while chronic mood symptoms and disorders, such as anxiety, can have deleterious effects on cognition in normal aging, especially with regard to learning and memory (Joels et al., 2006; McEwen & Sapolsky, 1995), the effects of anxiety can further exacerbate the process of cognitive decline. Specifically, state anxiety can impact working memory capacity, multitasking, processing speed, and learning, while trait anxiety predisposes older adults to cognitive effects of distractibility, poor response inhibition, problem solving, and sustained attention. Further, these reductions can in turn lead to profound limitations in instrumental activities of daily living.

Lastly addressed in this chapter are the interventions that are available to treat anxiety, namely psychotherapy, psychotropic and medical interventions, stress reduction (e.g., mindfulness; leisure), physical exercise, cognitive training and rehabilitation, and brain healthy diet, that can combat its effects, and aim to lessen the severity in which both state and trait anxiety can impact cognitive functioning in older adults.

REFERENCES

2014 Alzheimer's disease facts and figures. (2014). Alzheimer's & Dementia: The Journal of the Alzheimer's Association, 10(2), e47-92.

Almeida, R. P., Schultz, S. A., Austin, B. P., Boots, E. A., Dowling, N. M., Gleason, C. E., . . . Okonkwo, O. C. (2015). Effect of cognitive reserve on age-related changes in cerebrospinal fluid biomarkers of Alzheimer

Disease. JAMA Neurology, 72(6), 699-706. doi: 10.1001/jamaneurol. 2015.0098.

Ayers, C. R., Sorrell, J. T., Thorp, S. R. and Wetherell, J. L. (2007). Evidence-based psychological treatments for late-life anxiety. Psychology and Aging, 22(1), 8-17. doi: 10.1037/0882-7974.22.1.8.

Backman, L., Jones, S., Berger, A. K., Laukka, E. J. and Small, B. J. (2005). Cognitive impairment in preclinical Alzheimer's disease: A meta-analysis. Neuropsychology, 19(4), 520-531. doi: 10.1037/0894-4105.19.4.520.

Backman, L. and Small, B. J. (2007). Cognitive deficits in preclinical Alzheimer's disease and vascular dementia: Patterns of findings from the Kungsholmen Project. Physiology & Behavior, 92(1-2), 80-86. doi: 10.1016/j.physbeh.2007.05.014.

Bandelow, B., Zohar, J., Hollander, E., Kasper, S., Moller, H. J., Zohar, J., . . . Vega, J. (2008). World Federation of Societies of Biological Psychiatry (WFSBP) guidelines for the pharmacological treatment of anxiety, obsessive-compulsive and post-traumatic stress disorders - first revision. The World Journal of Biological Psychiatry, 9(4), 248-312. doi: 10.1080/15622970802465807.

Bar-Haim, Y., Kerem, A., Lamy, D. and Zakay, D. (2010). When time slows down: The influence of threat on time perception in anxiety. Cognition and Emotion, 24(2), 255-263.

Barisa, M. (2014). Mood disorders: Mania, depression, and anxiety. In K. J. Stucky, M. W. Kirkwood & J. Donders (Eds.), Neuropsychology Study Guide and Board Review (pp. 519-543). New York: Oxford University Press.

Barlow, D. H. (2004). Anxiety and its disorders: The nature and treatment of anxiety and panic: Guilford press.

Barlow, D. H., Farchione, T. J., Fairholme, C. P., Ellard, K. K., Boisseau, C. L., Allen, L. B. and May, J. T. E. (2010). Unified protocol for transdiagnostic treatment of emotional disorders: Therapist guide: Oxford University Press, USA.

Barnes, D. E., Yaffe, K., Belfor, N., Jagust, W. J., DeCarli, C., Reed, B. R. and Kramer, J. H. (2009). Computer-based cognitive training for mild cognitive impairment: results from a pilot randomized, controlled trial. Alzheimer Disease and Associated Disorders, 23(3), 205-210. doi: 10.1097/WAD.0b013e31819c6137.

Barrowclough, C., King, P., Colville, J., Russell, E., Burns, A. and Tarrier, N. (2001). A randomized trial of the effectiveness of cognitive-behavioral therapy and supportive counseling for anxiety symptoms in older adults. Journal of Consulting and Clinical Psychology, 69(5), 756-762.

Baxter, M. G., Parker, A., Lindner, C. C., Izquierdo, A. D. and Murray, E. A. (2000). Control of response selection by reinforcer value requires interaction of amygdala and orbital prefrontal cortex. The Journal of Neuroscience, 20(11), 4311-4319.

Beauchet, O., Launay, C. P., Annweiler, C. and Allali, G. (2015). Hippocampal volume, early cognitive decline and gait variability: which association? Experimental Gerontology, 61, 98-104. doi: 10.1016/j.exger.2014.11.002.

Beaudreau, S. A. and O'Hara, R. (2008). Late-life anxiety and cognitive impairment: a review. The American Journal of Geriatric Psychiatry, 16(10), 790-803. doi: 10.1097/JGP.0b013e31817945c3.

Beck, C. T. (1995). The effects of postpartum depression on maternal-infant interaction: a meta-analysis. Nursing Research, 44(5), 298-304.

Beck, J. G., Stanley, M. A. and Zebb, B. J. (1996). Characteristics of generalized anxiety disorder in older adults: a descriptive study. Behaviour Research and Therapy, 34(3), 225-234.

Beekman, A. T., Deeg, D. J., van Tilburg, T., Smit, J. H., Hooijer, C. and van Tilburg, W. (1995). Major and minor depression in later life: a study of prevalence and risk factors. Journal of Affective Disorders, 36(1-2), 65-75.

Berggren, N. and Derakshan, N. (2013). Attentional control deficits in trait anxiety: Why you see them and why you don't. Biological Psychology, 92(3), 440-446. doi: 10.1016/j.biopsycho.2012.03.007.

Black, D. S., O'Reilly, G. A., Olmstead, R., Breen, E. C. and Irwin, M. R. (2015). Mindfulness meditation and improvement in sleep quality and daytime impairment among older adults with sleep disturbances: A randomized clinical trial. JAMA Internal Medicine, 175(4), 494-501. doi: 10.1001/jamainternmed.2014.8081.

Blazer, D. G. (2002). Self-efficacy and depression in late life: a primary prevention proposal. Aging and Mental Health, 6(4), 315-324. doi: 10.1080/1360786021000006938.

Booth, J. E., Schinka, J. A., Brown, L. M., Mortimer, J. A. and Borenstein, A. R. (2006). Five-factor personality dimensions, mood states, and cognitive performance in older adults. Journal of Clinical and Experimental Neuropsychology, 28(5), 676-683. doi: 10.1080/13803390590954209.

Bourne, E. L. (2005). The anxiety & phobia workbook (4th ed.). Oakland, CA: New Harbinger Publications.

Braaten, A. J., Parsons, T. D., McCue, R., Sellers, A. and Burns, W. J. (2006). Neurocognitive differential diagnosis of dementing diseases: Alzheimer's Dementia, Vascular Dementia, Frontotemporal Dementia, and Major Depressive Disorder. The International Journal of Neuroscience, 116(11), 1271-1293. doi: 10.1080/00207450600920928.

Brenes, G. A., Guralnik, J. M., Williamson, J. D., Fried, L. P., Simpson, C., Simonsick, E. M. and Penninx, B. W. (2005). The influence of anxiety on the progression of disability. Journal of American Geriatrics Society, 53(1), 34-39. doi: 10.1111/j.1532-5415.2005.53007.x.

Bryant, C., Jackson, H. and Ames, D. (2008). The prevalence of anxiety in older adults: methodological issues and a review of the literature. Journal of Affective Disorders, 109(3), 233-250. doi: 10.1016/j.jad.2007.11.008.

Burke, H. M., Davis, M. C., Otte, C. and Mohr, D. C. (2005). Depression and cortisol responses to psychological stress: a meta-analysis. Psychoneuroendocrinology, 30(9), 846-856. doi: 10.1016/j.psyneuen. 2005.02.010.

Bush, S. S. (2014). Psychological Assessment of Veterans: Oxford University Press.

Byers, A. L., Yaffe, K., Covinsky, K. E., Friedman, M. B. and Bruce, M. L. (2010). High occurrence of mood and anxiety disorders among older adults: The National Comorbidity Survey Replication. Archives of General Psychiatry, 67(5), 489-496. doi: 10.1001/archgen psychiatry.2010.35.

Byrne, A. and Byrne, D. G. (1993). The effect of exercise on depression, anxiety and other mood states: A review. Journal of Psychosomatic Research, 37(6), 565-574.

Byron, K. and Khazanchi, S. (2011). A meta-analytic investigation of the relationship of state and trait anxiety to performance on figural and verbal creative tasks. Personality and Social Psychology Bulletin, 37(2), 269-283. doi: 10.1177/0146167210392788.

Bystritsky, A., Khalsa, S. S., Cameron, M. E. and Schiffman, J. (2013). Current diagnosis and treatment of anxiety disorders. P & T: a peer-reviewed journal for formulary management, 38(1), 30-57.

Caselli, R. J., Dueck, A. C., Osborne, D., Sabbagh, M. N., Connor, D. J., Ahern, G. L., . . . Reiman, E. M. (2009). Longitudinal modeling of age-related memory decline and the APOE epsilon4 effect. The New England Journal of Medicine, 361(3), 255-263. doi: 10.1056/NEJMoa0809437.

Cassidy, K. and Rector, N. A. (2008). The silent geriatric giant: Anxiety disorders in late life. Geriatrics and Aging, 11(3), 150-156.

Cayre, M., Malaterre, J., Scotto-Lomassese, S., Strambi, C. and Strambi, A. (2002). The common properties of neurogenesis in the adult brain: from invertebrates to vertebrates. Comparative Biochemistry and Physiology Part B: Biochemistry and Molecular Biology, 132(1), 1-15.

Chamberlain, S. R., Muller, U., Deakin, J. B., Corlett, P. R., Dowson, J., Cardinal, R. N., . . . Sahakian, B. J. (2007). Lack of deleterious effects of buspirone on cognition in healthy male volunteers. Journal of Psychopharmacology, 21(2), 210-215. doi: 10.1177/0269881107068066.

Charney, D. S. (2003). Neuroanatomical circuits modulating fear and anxiety behaviors. Acta Psychiatrica Scandinavica Supplementum (417), 38-50.

Cicerone, K. D., Dahlberg, C., Kalmar, K., Langenbahn, D. M., Malec, J. F., Bergquist, T. F., . . . Morse, P. A. (2000). Evidence-based cognitive rehabilitation: recommendations for clinical practice. Archives of Physical Medicine and Rehabilitation, 81(12), 1596-1615. doi: 10.1053/apmr.2000.19240.

Cohen, D., Eisdorfer, C., Vitaliano, P. P. and Bloom, V. (1980). The relationship of age, anxiety, and serum immunoglobulins with crystallized and fluid intelligence. Biological Psychiatry, 15(5), 699-709.

Colcombe, S. and Kramer, A. F. (2003). Fitness effects on the cognitive function of older adults: A meta-analytic study. Psychological Science, 14(2), 125-130.

Cole, M. G. and Dendukuri, N. (2003). Risk factors for depression among elderly community subjects: A systematic review and meta-analysis. The American Journal of Psychiatry, 160(6), 1147-1156. doi: 10.1176/appi.ajp.160.6.1147.

Cook, J. M., Biyanova, T., Masci, C. and Coyne, J. C. (2007). Older patient perspectives on long-term anxiolytic benzodiazepine use and discontinuation: A qualitative study. Journal of General Internal Medicine, 22(8), 1094-1100. doi: 10.1007/s11606-007-0205-5.

Cotman, C. W. and Berchtold, N. C. (2002). Exercise: A behavioral intervention to enhance brain health and plasticity. Trends in Neurosciences, 25(6), 295-301.

Craske, M. G., Roy-Byrne, P. P., Stein, M. B., Sullivan, G., Sherbourne, C. and Bystritsky, A. (2009). Treatment for anxiety disorders: Efficacy to effectiveness to implementation. Behaviour Research and Therapy, 47(11), 931-937. doi: 10.1016/j.brat.2009.07.012.

Crowley, K. (2011). Sleep and sleep disorders in older adults. Neuropsychology Review, 21(1), 41-53. doi: 10.1007/s11065-010-9154-6.

Cullum, C. and Liff, C. (2014). Mild cognitive impairment and Alzheimer's disease. In M. Stucky, M. Kirkwood & J. Donders (Eds.), Clinical neuropsychology study guide and board review (pp. 108-116): Oxford University Press.

Cummings, J. L. and Benson, D. F. (1992). Dementia: A clinical approach: Butterworth-Heinemann Medical.

Cummings, J. L., Benson, D. F. and Levine, S. (1984). Dementia: A clinical approach. Journal of Neuropathology & Experimental Neurology, 43(6), 657.

Dai, J., Buijs, R. and Swaab, D. (2004). Glucocorticoid hormone (cortisol) affects axonal transport in human cortex neurons but shows resistance in Alzheimer's disease. British Journal of Pharmacology, 143(5), 606-610. doi: 10.1038/sj.bjp.0705995.

Damasio, A. R., Tranel, D. and Damasio, H. (1990). Individuals with sociopathic behavior caused by frontal damage fail to respond autonomically to social stimuli. Behavioral Brain Research, 41(2), 81-94.

Deptula, D., Singh, R. and Pomara, N. (1993). Aging, emotional states, and memory. The American Journal of Psychiatry, 150(3), 429-434. doi: 10.1176/ajp.150.3.429.

Dunn, A. L., Trivedi, M. H. and O'Neal, H. A. (2001). Physical activity dose-response effects on outcomes of depression and anxiety. Medicine and Science in Sports and Exercise, 33(6 Suppl), S587-597; discussion 609-510.

Edwards, M. S., Moore, P., Champion, J. C. and Edwards, E. J. (2015). Effects of trait anxiety and situational stress on attentional shifting are buffered by working memory capacity. Anxiety, Stress, and Coping, 28(1), 1-16. doi: 10.1080/10615806.2014.911846.

Endler, N. S., Kantor, L. and Parker, J. D. A. (1994). State-trait coping, state-trait anxiety and academic performance. Personality and Individual Differences, 16(5), 663-670. doi: 10.1016/0191-8869(94)90208-9.

Endler, N. S. and Kocovski, N. L. (2001). State and trait anxiety revisited. Journal of Anxiety Disorders, 15(3), 231-245.

Ewers, M., Insel, P. S., Stern, Y. and Weiner, M. W. (2013). Cognitive reserve associated with FDG-PET in preclinical Alzheimer disease. Neurology, 80(13), 1194-1201. doi: 10.1212/WNL.0b013e31828970c2.

Eysenck, M. W., Derakshan, N., Santos, R. and Calvo, M. G. (2007). Anxiety and cognitive performance: Attentional control theory. Emotion, 7(2), 336-353. doi: 10.1037/1528-3542.7.2.336.

Farach, F. J., Pruitt, L. D., Jun, J. J., Jerud, A. B., Zoellner, L. A. and Roy-Byrne, P. P. (2012). Pharmacological treatment of anxiety disorders: current treatments and future directions. Journal of Anxiety Disorders, 26(8), 833-843. doi: 10.1016/j.janxdis.2012.07.009.

Ferri, C. P., Prince, M., Brayne, C., Brodaty, H., Fratiglioni, L., Ganguli, M., . . . Scazufca, M. (2005). Global prevalence of dementia: A Delphi consensus study. Lancet, 366(9503), 2112-2117. doi: 10.1016/S0140-6736(05)67889-0.

Flint, A. J. (1994). Epidemiology and comorbidity of anxiety disorders in the elderly. The American Journal of Psychiatry, 151(5), 640-649.

Fries, E., Hesse, J., Hellhammer, J. and Hellhammer, D. H. (2005). A new view on hypocortisolism. Psychoneuroendocrinology, 30(10), 1010-1016. doi: 10.1016/j.psyneuen.2005.04.006.

Fusco, D., Colloca, G., Monaco, M. R. L. and Cesari, M. (2007). Effects of antioxidant supplementation on the aging process. Clinical Interverntions in Aging, 2(3), 377-387.

Gautam, M., Agrawal, M., Gautam, M., Sharma, P., Gautam, A. S. and Gautam, S. (2012). Role of antioxidants in generalised anxiety disorder and depression. Indian Journal of Psychiatry, 54(3), 244-247. doi: 10.4103/0019-5545.102424.

Goodwin, J. (1983). Common psychiatric disorders in elderly persons. The Western Journal of Medicine, 139(4), 502-506.

Green, C. S. and Bavelier, D. (2008). Exercising your brain: A review of human brain plasticity and training-induced learning. Psychology and Aging, 23(4), 692-701. doi: 10.1037/a0014345.

Greenwood, P. M. (2000). The frontal aging hypothesis evaluated. Journal of the International Neuropsychological Society, 6(6), 705-726.

Grossman, P., Niemann, L., Schmidt, S. and Walach, H. (2004). Mindfulness-based stress reduction and health benefits. A meta-analysis. Journal of Psychosomatic Research, 57(1), 35-43. doi: 10.1016/S0022-3999(03)00573-7.

Gurland, B. J., Dean, L. L., Copeland, J., Gurland, R. and Golden, R. (1982). Criteria for the diagnosis of dementia in the community elderly. The Gerontologist, 22(2), 180-186.

Gutierrez, J. and Isaacson, R. S. (2013). Prevention of cognitive decline. In L. D. Ravdin & H. L. Katzen (Eds.), Handbook on the neuropsychology of aging and dementia (pp. 167-192). New York: Springer.

Gutteling, B. M., de Weerth, C. and Buitelaar, J. K. (2005). Prenatal stress and children's cortisol reaction to the first day of school.

Psychoneuroendocrinology, 30(6), 541-549. doi: 10.1016/j.psyneuen. 2005.01.002.

Guttmann, C. R., Jolesz, F. A., Kikinis, R., Killiany, R. J., Moss, M. B., Sandor, T. and Albert, M. S. (1998). White matter changes with normal aging. Neurology, 50(4), 972-978.

Halligan, S. L., Herbert, J., Goodyer, I. and Murray, L. (2007). Disturbances in morning cortisol secretion in association with maternal postnatal depression predict subsequent depressive symptomatology in adolescents. Biological Psychiatry, 62(1), 40-46. doi: 10.1016/j.biopsych.2006.09.011.

Hebert, R. and Brayne, C. (1995). Epidemiology of vascular dementia. Neuroepidemiology, 14(5), 240-257.

Hofmann, S. G., Sawyer, A. T., Witt, A. A. and Oh, D. (2010). The effect of mindfulness-based therapy on anxiety and depression: A meta-analytic review. Journal of Consulting and Clinical Psychology, 78(2), 169-183. doi: 10.1037/a0018555.

Hogan, C. L., Mata, J. and Carstensen, L. L. (2013). Exercise holds immediate benefits for affect and cognition in younger and older adults. Psychology and Aging, 28(2), 587-594. doi: 10.1037/a0032634.

Huntley, J. D., Gould, R. L., Liu, K., Smith, M. and Howard, R. J. (2015). Do cognitive interventions improve general cognition in dementia? A meta-analysis and meta-regression. BMJ Open, 5(4), e005247. doi: 10.1136/bmjopen-2014-005247.

Joels, M., Pu, Z., Wiegert, O., Oitzl, M. S. and Krugers, H. J. (2006). Learning under stress: How does it work? Trends in Cognitive Sciences, 10(4), 152-158. doi: 10.1016/j.tics.2006.02.002.

Kakimoto, A., Ito, S., Okada, H., Nishizawa, S., Minoshima, S. and Ouchi, Y. (2015). Age-related gender-specific changes in the brain metabolism and morphology. Journal of Nuclear Medicine. doi: 10.2967/jnumed. 115.166439.

Kravitz, J., Kim, J., Faust-Socher, A., Rogers, S. and Miller, K. (2008). Mild cognitive impairment: Current trends for early detection and treatment. In H. S. Jeong (Ed.), Alzheimer's disease in the middle-aged (pp. 1-66). Hauppauge, NY: Nova Biomedical Books.

Kukull, W. A., Higdon, R., Bowen, J. D., McCormick, W. C., Teri, L., Schellenberg, G. D., . . . Larson, E. B. (2002). Dementia and Alzheimer disease incidence: A prospective cohort study. Archives of Neurology, 59(11), 1737-1746.

LaRue, A. and D'Elia, L. F. (1985). Anxiety and problem solving in middle-aged and elderly adults. Experimental Aging Research, 11(3-4), 215-220. doi: 10.1080/03610738508259190.

Leitner, M. J. and Leitner, S. F. (2012). Leisure in later life (4 ed.). New York: Haworth Press.

Lenehan, M. E., Summers, M. J., Saunders, N. L., Summers, J. J., Ward, D. D., Ritchie, K. and Vickers, J. C. (2015). Sending Your Grandparents to University Increases Cognitive Reserve: The Tasmanian Healthy Brain Project. Neuropsychology. doi: 10.1037/neu0000249.

Leung, G. T., Leung, K. F. and Lam, L. C. (2011). Classification of late-life leisure activities among elderly Chinese in Hong Kong. East Asian Archives of Psychiatry, 21(3), 123-127.

Liepelt-Scarfone, I., Fruhmann Berger, M., Prakash, D., Csoti, I., Graber, S., Maetzler, W. and Berg, D. (2013). Clinical characteristics with an impact on ADL functions of PD patients with cognitive impairment indicative of dementia. PLoS One, 8(12), e82902. doi: 10.1371/journal.pone.0082902.

Lindsey, P. L. (2009). Psychotropic medication use among older adults: What all nurses need to know. Journal of Gerontological Nursing, 35(9), 28-38. doi: 10.3928/00989134-20090731-01.

Liu, R. S., Lemieux, L., Bell, G. S., Sisodiya, S. M., Shorvon, S. D., Sander, J. W. and Duncan, J. S. (2003). A longitudinal study of brain morphometrics using quantitative magnetic resonance imaging and difference image analysis. Neuroimage, 20(1), 22-33.

Llorente, M. D., David, D., Golden, A. G. and Silverman, M. A. (2000). Defining patterns of benzodiazepine use in older adults. Journal of Geriatric Psychiatry and Neurology, 13(3), 150-160.

Lobo, V., Patil, A., Phatak, A. and Chandra, N. (2010). Free radicals, antioxidants and functional foods: Impact on human health. Pharmacognosy Reviews, 4(8), 118-126. doi: 10.4103/0973-7847.70902.

Lopez, M. E., Aurtenetxe, S., Pereda, E., Cuesta, P., Castellanos, N. P., Bruna, R., . . . Bajo, R. (2014). Cognitive reserve is associated with the functional organization of the brain in healthy aging: A MEG study. Frontiers in Aging Neuroscience, 6, 125. doi: 10.3389/fnagi.2014.00125.

Lupien, S. J., de Leon, M., de Santi, S., Convit, A., Tarshish, C., Nair, N. P., . . . Meaney, M. J. (1998). Cortisol levels during human aging predict hippocampal atrophy and memory deficits. Nature Neuroscience, 1(1), 69-73. doi: 10.1038/271.

Lupien, S. J., King, S., Meaney, M. J. and McEwen, B. S. (2000). Child's stress hormone levels correlate with mother's socioeconomic status and depressive state. Biological Psychiatry, 48(10), 976-980.

Lupien, S. J., McEwen, B. S., Gunnar, M. R. and Heim, C. (2009). Effects of stress throughout the lifespan on the brain, behaviour and cognition. Nature Reviews Neuroscience, 10(6), 434-445. doi: 10.1038/nrn2639.

Lyons-Ruth, K., Wolfe, R. and Lyubchik, A. (2000). Depression and the parenting of young children: making the case for early preventive mental health services. Harvard Review of Psychiatry, 8(3), 148-153.

Magnusson, D. (1980). Trait-state anxiety: a note on conceptual and empirical relationships. Personality and Individual Differences, 1(3), 215-217.

Mantella, R. C., Butters, M. A., Dew, M. A., Mulsant, B. H., Begley, A. E., Tracey, B., . . . Lenze, E. J. (2007). Cognitive impairment in late-life generalized anxiety disorder. The American Journal of Geriatric Psychiatry, 15(8), 673-679. doi: 10.1097/JGP.0b013e31803111f2.

Marciniak, R., Sheardova, K., Cermakova, P., Hudecek, D., Sumec, R. and Hort, J. (2014). Effect of meditation on cognitive functions in context of aging and neurodegenerative diseases. Frontiers in Behavioral Neuroscience, 8, 17. doi: 10.3389/fnbeh.2014.00017.

Martella, D., Casagrande, M. and Lupianez, J. (2011). Alerting, orienting and executive control: The effects of sleep deprivation on attentional networks. Experimental Brain Research, 210(1), 81-89. doi: 10.1007/s00221-011-2605-3.

Mather, M. (2012). The emotion paradox in the aging brain. Annals of the New York Academy of Sciences, 1251, 33-49. doi: 10.1111/j.1749-6632.2012.06471.x.

Mathews, A., Fox, E., Yiend, J. and Calder, A. (2003). The face of fear: Effects of eye gaze and emotion on visual attention. Visual Cognition, 10(7), 823-835. doi: 10.1080/13506280344000095.

McEwen, B. S. and Sapolsky, R. M. (1995). Stress and cognitive function. Current Opinion in Neurobiology, 5(2), 205-216.

McGowan, P. O., Sasaki, A., D'Alessio, A. C., Dymov, S., Labonte, B., Szyf, M., . . . Meaney, M. J. (2009). Epigenetic regulation of the glucocorticoid receptor in human brain associates with childhood abuse. Nature Neuroscience, 12(3), 342-348. doi: 10.1038/nn.2270.

McTeague, L. M., Shumen, J. R., Wieser, M. J., Lang, P. J. and Keil, A. (2011). Social vision: Sustained perceptual enhancement of affective facial cues in social anxiety. Neuroimage, 54(2), 1615-1624. doi: 10.1016/j.neuroimage. 2010.08.080.

Mendez, M. F., Lauterbach, E. C. and Sampson, S. M. (2008). An evidence-based review of the psychopathology of frontotemporal dementia: A report of the ANPA Committee on Research. The Journal of Neuropsychiatry and Clinical Neurosciences, 20(2), 130-149.

Mendez, M. F. and Perryman, K. M. (2002). Neuropsychiatric features of frontotemporal dementia: Evaluation of consensus criteria and review. The Journal of Neuropsychiatry and Clinical Neurosciences, 14(4), 424-429. doi: 10.1176/jnp.14.4.424.

Miller, K., Ercoli, L., Kim, J. and Small, G. W. (2010). Memory Training for Older Adults. Principles and Practice of Geriatric Psychiatry, 397-402.

Miller, K. J., Siddarth, P., Gaines, J. M., Parrish, J. M., Ercoli, L. M., Marx, K., . . . Small, G. W. (2012). The memory fitness program: Cognitive effects of a healthy aging intervention. The American Journal of Geriatric Psychiatry, 20(6), 514-523. doi: 10.1097/JGP.0b013e318227f821.

Mitte, K., Noack, P., Steil, R. and Hautzinger, M. (2005). A meta-analytic review of the efficacy of drug treatment in generalized anxiety disorder. Journal of Clinical Psychopharmacology, 25(2), 141-150.

Mohlman, J. (2013). Older Adults Overwhelmingly Prefer Psychotherapy for the Treatment of Anxiety. Clinician's Research Digest: Adult Populations, 31(3), 3-3. doi: 10.1037/e525102013-005.

Mokhber, N., Azarpazhooh, M. R., Khajehdaluee, M., Velayati, A. and Hopwood, M. (2010). Randomized, single-blind, trial of sertraline and buspirone for treatment of elderly patients with generalized anxiety disorder. Psychiatry and Clinical Neurosciences, 64(2), 128-133. doi: 10.1111/j.1440-1819.2009.02055.x.

Murphy, M. and Mercer, J. G. (2013). Diet-regulated anxiety. International Journal of Endocrinology, 2013, 701967. doi: 10.1155/2013/701967.

Norton, J., Ancelin, M. L., Stewart, R., Berr, C., Ritchie, K. and Carriere, I. (2012). Anxiety symptoms and disorder predict activity limitations in the elderly. Journal of Affective Disorders, 141(2-3), 276-285. doi: 10.1016/j.jad.2012.04.002.

O'Connor, T. G., Ben-Shlomo, Y., Heron, J., Golding, J., Adams, D. and Glover, V. (2005). Prenatal anxiety predicts individual differences in cortisol in pre-adolescent children. Biological Psychiatry, 58(3), 211-217. doi: 10.1016/j.biopsych.2005.03.032.

Orellana, C., Ferreira, D., Muehlboeck, J. S., Mecocci, P., Vellas, B., Tsolaki, M., . . . Westman, E. (2016). Measuring Global Brain Atrophy with the Brain Volume/Cerebrospinal Fluid Index: Normative Values, Cut-Offs and Clinical Associations. Neuro-degenerative Diseases, 16(1-2), 77-86. doi: 10.1159/000442443.

Pacheco-Unguetti, A. P., Acosta, A., Callejas, A. and Lupianez, J. (2010). Attention and anxiety: Different attentional functioning under state and trait anxiety. Psychological Science, 21(2), 298-304. doi: 10.1177/0956797609359624.

Panza, F., Solfrizzi, V., Colacicco, A. M., D'Introno, A., Capurso, C., Torres, F., . . . Capurso, A. (2004). Mediterranean diet and cognitive decline. Public Health Nutrition, 7(7), 959-963.

Park, D. C. and Reuter-Lorenz, P. (2009). The adaptive brain: aging and neurocognitive scaffolding. Annual Review of Psychology, 60, 173-196. doi: 10.1146/annurev.psych.59.103006.093656.

Paterniti, S., Dufouil, C., Bisserbe, J. C. and Alperovitch, A. (1999). Anxiety, depression, psychotropic drug use and cognitive impairment. Psychological Medicine, 29(2), 421-428.

Patterson, I. (1996). Participation in leisure activities by older adults after a stressful life event: The loss of a spouse. International Journal of Aging & Human Development, 42(2), 123-142.

Persson, C. M., Wallin, A. K., Levander, S. and Minthon, L. (2009). Changes in cognitive domains during three years in patients with Alzheimer's disease treated with donepezil. BMC Neurology, 9, 7. doi: 10.1186/1471-2377-9-7.

Petersen, R. C. (2006). Conversion. Neurology, 67(9 suppl 3), S12-S13.

Petersen, R. C. (2007). Mild cognitive impairment: current research and clinical implications. Seminars in Neurology, 27(1), 22-31. doi: 10.1055/s-2006-956752.

Petersen, R. C., Doody, R., Kurz, A., Mohs, R. C., Morris, J. C., Rabins, P. V., . . . Winblad, B. (2001). Current concepts in mild cognitive impairment. Archives of Neurology, 58(12), 1985-1992.

Petersen, R. C. and O'Brien, J. (2006). Mild cognitive impairment should be considered for DSM-V. Journal of Geriatric Psychiatry and Neurology, 19(3), 147-154. doi: 10.1177/0891988706291085.

Petersen, R. C., Smith, G. E., Waring, S. C., Ivnik, R. J., Kokmen, E. and Tangelos, E. G. (1997). Aging, memory, and mild cognitive impairment. International Psychogeriatriatrics, 9 Suppl 1, 65-69.

Pietrzak, R. H., Lim, Y. Y., Neumeister, A., Ames, D., Ellis, K. A., Harrington, K., . . . Maruff, P. (2015). Amyloid-beta, anxiety, and cognitive decline in preclinical Alzheimer disease: a multicenter, prospective cohort study. JAMA Psychiatry, 72(3), 284-291. doi: 10.1001/jamapsychiatry.2014.2476.

Pinquart, M. and Duberstein, P. R. (2007). Treatment of anxiety disorders in older adults: A meta-analytic comparison behavioral and pharmacological interventions. The American Journal of Geriatric Psychiatry, 15(8), 639-651. doi: 10.1097/JGP.0b013e31806841c8.

Pruessner, J. C., Baldwin, M. W., Dedovic, K., Renwick, R., Mahani, N. K., Lord, C., . . . Lupien, S. (2005). Self-esteem, locus of control, hippocampal volume, and cortisol regulation in young and old adulthood. Neuroimage, 28(4), 815-826. doi: 10.1016/j.neuroimage.2005.06.014.

Reiss, S. (1997). Trait anxiety: it's not what you think it is. Journal of Anxiety Disorders, 11(2), 201-214.

Reuter-Lorenz, P. A. and Park, D. C. (2010). Human neuroscience and the aging mind: a new look at old problems. The Journals of Gerontology Series B: Psychological Sciences and Social Sciences, 65(4), 405-415. doi: 10.1093/geronb/gbq035.

Rizzi, L., Rosset, I. and Roriz-Cruz, M. (2014). Global epidemiology of dementia: Alzheimer's and vascular types. Biomed Research International, 2014, 908915. doi: 10.1155/2014/908915.

Rodda, J., Boyce, N. and Walker, Z. (2008). The old age psychiatry handbook: a practical guide: John Wiley & Sons.

Rogers, S. A., Kang, C. H. and Miller, K. J. (2007). Cognitive profiles of aging and aging-related conditions.

Salthouse, T. (2009). Major issues in cognitive aging: Oxford University Press.

Salthouse, T. A. (1996). The processing-speed theory of adult age differences in cognition. Psychological Review, 103(3), 403-428.

Salthouse, T. A., Atkinson, T. M. and Berish, D. E. (2003). Executive functioning as a potential mediator of age-related cognitive decline in normal adults. Journal of Experimental Psychology: General, 132(4), 566-594. doi: 10.1037/0096-3445.132.4.566.

Salthouse, T. A. and Babcock, R. L. (1991). Decomposing adult age differences in working memory. Developmental Psychology, 27(5), 763.

Sapolsky, R. M. (1996). Why stress is bad for your brain. Science (New York, N.Y.), 273(5276), 749-750.

Satz, P. (1993). Brain reserve capacity on symptom onset after brain injury: A formulation and review of evidence for threshold theory. Neuropsychology, 7(3), 273.

Scahill, R. I., Frost, C., Jenkins, R., Whitwell, J. L., Rossor, M. N. and Fox, N. C. (2003). A longitudinal study of brain volume changes in normal aging using serial registered magnetic resonance imaging. Archives of Neurology, 60(7), 989-994. doi: 10.1001/archneur.60.7.989.

Scrable, H., Burns-Cusato, M. and Medrano, S. (2009). Anxiety and the aging brain: Stressed out over p53? Biochimica et Biophysica Acta, 1790(12), 1587-1591. doi: 10.1016/j.bbagen.2009.09.007.

Shimada-Sugimoto, M., Otowa, T. and Hettema, J. M. (2015). Genetics of anxiety disorders: Genetic epidemiological and molecular studies in humans. Psychiatry and Clinical Neurosciences, 69(7), 388-401. doi: 10.1111/pcn.12291.

Shineman, D. W., Salthouse, T. A., Launer, L. J., Hof, P. R., Bartzokis, G., Kleiman, R., . . . Fillit, H. M. (2010). Therapeutics for cognitive aging. Annals of the New York Academy of Sciences, 1191 Suppl 1, E1-15. doi: 10.1111/j.1749-6632.2010.05532.x.

Sinoff, G. and Werner, P. (2003). Anxiety disorder and accompanying subjective memory loss in the elderly as a predictor of future cognitive decline. International Journal of Geriatric Psychiatry, 18(10), 951-959. doi: 10.1002/gps.1004.

Small, G. W., La Rue, A., Komo, S., Kaplan, A. and Mandelkern, M. A. (1995). Predictors of cognitive change in middle-aged and older adults with memory loss. The American Journal of Psychiatry, 152(12), 1757-1764. doi: 10.1176/ajp.152.12.1757.

Small, G. W., Okonek, A., Mandelkern, M. A., La Rue, A., Chang, L., Khonsary, A., . . . Blahd, W. H. (1994). Age-associated memory loss: initial neuropsychological and cerebral metabolic findings of a longitudinal study. International Psychogeriatrics, 6(1), 23-44; discussion 60-22.

Small, S. A. (2001). Age-related memory decline: Current concepts and future directions. Archives of Neurology, 58(3), 360-364.

Smith, M. E. (2005). Bilateral hippocampal volume reduction in adults with post-traumatic stress disorder: a meta-analysis of structural MRI studies. Hippocampus, 15(6), 798-807. doi: 10.1002/hipo.20102.

Sohlberg, M. M. (2012). Cognitive rehabilitation manual: Translating evidence-based recommendations into practice. Archives of Clinical Neuropsychology, 27(8), 931-932.

Solfrizzi, V., Panza, F. and Capurso, A. (2003). The role of diet in cognitive decline. Journal of Neural Transmission, 110(1), 95-110. doi: 10.1007/s00702-002-0766-8.

Sorrell, J. M. (2015). Meditation for older adults: A new look at an ancient intervention for mental health. Journal of Psychosocial Nursing and Mental Health Services, 53(5), 15-19. doi: 10.3928/02793695-20150330-01.

Spaulding, W. D., Reed, D., Sullivan, M., Richardson, C. and Weiler, M. (1999). Effects of cognitive treatment in psychiatric rehabilitation. Schizophrenia Bulletin, 25(4), 657-676.

Spielberger, C. D., Gorsuch, R. L. and Lushene, R. E. (1970). Manual for the State-Trait Anxiety Inventory. Palo Alto: Consulting Psychologists Press.

Stanley, M. A., Wilson, N. L., Amspoker, A. B., Kraus-Schuman, C., Wagener, P. D., Calleo, J. S., . . . Kunik, M. E. (2014). Lay providers can deliver effective cognitive behavior therapy for older adults with generalized anxiety disorder: A randomized trial. Depression and Anxiety, 31(5), 391-401. doi: 10.1002/da.22239.

Stern, Y. (2012). Cognitive reserve in ageing and Alzheimer's disease. The Lancet Neurology, 11(11), 1006-1012. doi: 10.1016/S1474-4422(12)70191-6.

Swihart, A. (2014). Vascular dementia. In K. Stucky, M. Kirkwood & J. Donders (Eds.), Clinical neuropsychology study guide and board review (pp. 116-123): Oxford University Press.

Teachman, B. A. (2006). Aging and negative affect: the rise and fall and rise of anxiety and depression symptoms. Psychology and Aging, 21(1), 201-207. doi: 10.1037/0882-7974.21.1.201.

Tesky, V. A., Thiel, C., Banzer, W. and Pantel, J. (2011). Effects of a group program to increase cognitive performance through cognitively stimulating leisure activities in healthy older subjects. The Journal of Gerontopsychology and Geriatric Psychiatry, 24(2), 83-92. doi: doi:10.1024/1662-9647/a000035.

Thompson, P. M., Moussai, J., Zohoori, S., Goldkorn, A., Khan, A. A., Mega, M. S., . . . Toga, A. W. (1998). Cortical variability and asymmetry in normal aging and Alzheimer's disease. Cerebral Cortex, 8(6), 492-509.

Tinetti, M. E., Inouye, S. K., Gill, T. M. and Doucette, J. T. (1995). Shared risk factors for falls, incontinence, and functional dependence. Unifying the approach to geriatric syndromes. JAMA, 273(17), 1348-1353.

Tom, S. E., Hubbard, R. A., Crane, P. K., Haneuse, S. J., Bowen, J., McCormick, W. C., . . . Larson, E. B. (2015). Characterization of dementia and Alzheimer's disease in an older population: Updated incidence and life expectancy with and without dementia. American

Journal of Public Health, 105(2), 408-413. doi: 10.2105/AJPH.2014.301935.

van Praag, H., Christie, B. R., Sejnowski, T. J. and Gage, F. H. (1999). Running enhances neurogenesis, learning, and long-term potentiation in mice. Proceedings of the National Academy of Sciences of the United States of America, 96(23), 13427-13431.

Verstynen, T. D., Lynch, B., Miller, D. L., Voss, M. W., Prakash, R. S., Chaddock, L., . . . Erickson, K. I. (2012). Caudate nucleus volume mediates the link between cardiorespiratory fitness and cognitive flexibility in older adults. Journal of Aging Research, 2012.

Videbech, P. and Ravnkilde, B. (2004). Hippocampal volume and depression: a meta-analysis of MRI studies. The American Journal of Psychiatry, 161(11), 1957-1966. doi: 10.1176/appi.ajp.161.11.1957.

Vink, D., Aartsen, M. J. and Schoevers, R. A. (2008). Risk factors for anxiety and depression in the elderly: A review. Journal of Affective Disorders, 106(1-2), 29-44. doi: 10.1016/j.jad.2007.06.005.

Vouimba, R. M., Yaniv, D. and Richter-Levin, G. (2007). Glucocorticoid receptors and beta-adrenoceptors in basolateral amygdala modulate synaptic plasticity in hippocampal dentate gyrus, but not in area CA1. Neuropharmacology, 52(1), 244-252. doi: 10.1016/j.neuropharm. 2006.07.007.

Voyer, P. and Martin, L. S. (2003). Improving geriatric mental health nursing care: Making a case for going beyond psychotropic medications. International Journal of Mental Health Nursing, 12(1), 11-21.

Weih, M., Abu-Omar, K., Esselmann, H., Gelbrich, G., Lewczuk, P., Rutten, A., . . . Kornhuber, J. (2009). Physical activity and prevention of Alzheimer's dementia: Current evidence and feasibility of an interventional trial. Fortschritte der Neurologie-Psychiatrie, 77(3), 146-151. doi: 10.1055/s-0028-1109068.

Weih, M., Degirmenci, Ü., Kreil, S. and Kornhuber, J. (2010). Physical activity and Alzheimer’s disease: A meta-analysis of cohort studies. GeroPsych: The Journal of Gerontopsychology and Geriatric Psychiatry, 23(1), 17.

Weih, M., Wiltfang, J. and Kornhuber, J. (2007). Non-pharmacologic prevention of Alzheimer's disease: nutritional and life-style risk factors. Journal of Neural Transmission, 114(9), 1187-1197. doi: 10.1007/s00702-007-0704-x.

Wetherell, J. L., Afari, N., Ayers, C. R., Stoddard, J. A., Ruberg, J., Sorrell, J. T., . . . Patterson, T. L. (2011). Acceptance and Commitment Therapy for generalized anxiety disorder in older adults: A preliminary report. Behavior Therapy, 42(1), 127-134. doi: 10.1016/j.beth.2010.07.002.

Wetherell, J. L., Gatz, M. and Craske, M. G. (2003). Treatment of generalized anxiety disorder in older adults. Journal of Consulting and Clinical Psychology, 71(1), 31-40.

Wetherell, J. L., Reynolds, C. A., Gatz, M. and Pedersen, N. L. (2002). Anxiety, cognitive performance, and cognitive decline in normal aging. The Journals of Gerontology Series B: Psychological Sciences and Social Sciences, 57(3), P246-255.

Whalley, L. (2015). Understanding brain aging and dementia. New York: Columbia University Press.

Wolitzky-Taylor, K. B., Castriotta, N., Lenze, E. J., Stanley, M. A. and Craske, M. G. (2010). Anxiety disorders in older adults: a comprehensive review. Depression and Anxiety, 27(2), 190-211. doi: 10.1002/da.20653.

Xu, Y., Valentino, D. J., Scher, A. I., Dinov, I., White, L. R., Thompson, P. M., . . . Toga, A. W. (2008). Age effects on hippocampal structural changes in old men: The HAAS. Neuroimage, 40(3), 1003-1015. doi: 10.1016/j.neuroimage.2007.12.034.

Yehuda, R., Golier, J. A. and Kaufman, S. (2005). Circadian rhythm of salivary cortisol in Holocaust survivors with and without PTSD. The American Journal of Psychiatry, 162(5), 998-1000. doi: 10.1176/appi.ajp.162.5.998.

Yiend, J. (2010). The effects of emotion on attention: A review of attentional processing of emotional information. Cognition and Emotion, 24(1), 3-47.

Young, R. J. (1979). The effect of regular exercise on cognitive functioning and personality. Brittish Journal of Sports Medicine, 13(3), 110-117.

Biographical Sketches

Name: Cory E. (Burns) Harrison

Affiliations:
UCLA Longevity Center
David Geffen School of Medicine at UCLA
Semel Institute for Neuroscience & Human Behavior
Azusa Pacific University
School of Behavioral Health

Department of Graduate Psychology

Education:

PsyD. Candidate in Clinical Psychology (expected completion 6/2018)
Azusa Pacific University

M.A. in Clinical Psychology
Azusa Pacific University

Address:
Azusa Pacific University
School of Behavioral Health
Department of Graduate Psychology
901 E. Alosta Ave, PO BOX 7000
Azusa, CA 91702
charrison@mednet.ucla.edu

Research and Professional Experience:

Neuropsychological assessment of adults whose cognitive and psychiatric functioning has been compromised due to a neurological disease or trauma.

Examining the Correlates of Schizophrenia and Religious Affiliations as it impacts the mental, social, and psychological functioning.

Honors:

Willard F. Harley Outstanding Senior Award (2013)
Dean's Recognition for Academic Excellence (2014; 2015)

Grant funding implementation and training for TIPP (Trauma Informed Philippines Psychotherapy)

Publications Last Three Years:

Harrison, C. (2015). *Understanding Religious Symptomatology in Schizophrenia.* Paper to be presented at the 2015 American Psychological Association Convention as part of a Symposium, August, Toronto, Canada.

Harrison, C. and Rogers, S. A. (2014). *Effects of Exercise and Leisure: Personality, Mood and Frontal Executive Functioning Differences Between Older Adults and College-Aged Participants.* Paper presented at the 2015 International Neuropsychology Society Convention, Denver, Colorado.

Burns, C. and Rogers, S. A. (2013). *Understanding Religious Symptomatology in Schizophrenia.* Paper presented at the 2013 Major Honors Research Celebration, Westmont College.

Burns, C. and Rogers, S. A. (2013). *Importance of personal wellness: A study on the way exercise and leisure activities relate to memory functions and personality.* Poster presented at the 2013 American Psychological Association Convention, Hawaii.

Burns, C. and Rogers, S. A. (2013). *The differential effects of exercise and leisure on the personality, mood, and frontal executive functioning of younger and older adults.* Poster presented at the 2013 American Psychological Association Convention, Hawaii.

Burns, C. and Rogers, S. A. (2013). *Importance of personal wellness: How exercise and leisure activities relate to memory.* Poster presented at the 2013 International Neuropsychology Society Convention, Waikoloa, Hawaii.

Harrison, C. and Rogers, S. A. (2014). *Effects of Leisure on Cognition among Older Adults.* Poster presented at the 2015 International Neuropsychology Society Convention, Denver, Colorado.

Harrison, C. and Rogers, S. A. (2015). *Identifying the specific deficits in executive functioning within the cognitive profile of Parkinson's disease.* Poster submitted for presentation at the 2016 International Neuropsychology Society Convention, Boston, Massachusetts.

Harrison, C. and Rogers, S. A. (2016). Effects of Leisure on Cognition among Older Adults. *Manuscript in preparation.*

Lowe, C., **Harrison, C.**, Curiel, A. and Miller, K. (2016). The effect of subclinical hypothyroidism on mood and cognition in older adults. *Manuscript in preparation.*

Name: Pavel Y. Litvin

Affiliations:

UCLA Longevity Center

David Geffen School of Medicine at UCLA

Semel Institute for Neuroscience & Human Behavior

Fielding Graduate University
School of Psychology
Department of Clinical Psychology

Education:

Ph.D. Clinical Psychology, Neuropsychology Concentration (expected graduation 2018)

Fielding Graduate University, Santa Barbara, CA

M.A. in Psychology (Marriage and Family Therapy Emphasis)
Chapman University

Address:

Fielding Graduate University
2020 De La Vina Street
Santa Barbara, CA 93105
plitvin@mednet.ucla.edu

Research Experience:

Operated transcranial magnetic brain stimulation for a double blind clinical trial evaluating the impact of the treatment on subjects with bipolar depression, coordinated collaborative research projects regarding cognitive training efficacy between St. Petersburg University and UCLA, presented data on the effectiveness of reading intervention programs for school aged children, and presently designing a study that will evaluate the effects of an arts program on measures of problem solving, family functioning, and self-efficacy of abused children.

Professional Experience:

In addition to regularly administering and interpreting neuropsychological assessments of adults with compromised cognitive functioning and those enrolled in clinical trials, currently operate a private practice specializing in the treatment of anxiety disorders and obsessive-compulsive disorder.

Publications Last Three Years:

Litvin, P. Y., Ho, A., Romers, C., Gutierrez, E. and Jacquin, K. M. Reading practice factors enhance intervention effects for struggling readers. Poster presented at the American Psychological Association Annual Convention, Toronto, Canada, August 2015.

Ho, A., Romers, C., Gutierrez, E., Litvin, P. Y. and Jacquin, K. M. Initial reading level predicts post-intervention improvements in reading abilities. Poster presented at the American Psychological Association Annual Convention, Washington, D.C., August 2014.

Romers, C., Gutierrez, E., Ho, A., Litvin, P. Y. and Jacquin, K. M. Intervention factors affecting changes in reading abilities in students enrolled in grades 2-12. Poster presented at the American Psychological Association Annual Convention, Washington, D.C., August 2014.

Spicer, S., Litvin, P.Y. and Soper, H. V. (in progress). Cognitive functioning of right hemisphere functioning for ages 4 to 8.

Sherwood, K., Litvin, P.Y. and Soper, H. V. (in progress). Relationship between moral reasoning and neuropsychological functions of executive and gestaltic processing.

Name: Rachel Lavian, M.A.

Affiliation:
UCLA Longevity Center
David Geffen School of Medicine at UCLA
Semel Institute for Neuroscience & Human Behavior

Alliant International University
California School of Professional Psychology

Education:
PhD Candidate in Clinical Psychology (expected completion 6/2017)
Alliant International University – CSPP

M.A. in Clinical Psychology
Alliant International University – CSPP

Address:
Alliant International University
California School of Professional Psychology
1000 S. Fremont Ave., Alhambra, CA 91803
rachellavian@mednet.ucla.edu

Research and Professional Experience:

Neuropsychological effects of neurological disease or trauma, effects of pomegranate, curcumin, or past cannabis use on cognition, vascular risk factors of cognitive decline, effects of gene on cognition, brain fitness, effects of subclinical depression on cognition

Honors:

Dean's Honors

Publications Last Three Years:

Name: Suranee A. Waleszonia

Affiliations:
UCLA Longevity Center
David Geffen School of Medicine at UCLA
Semel Institute for Neuroscience & Human Behavior

Loma Linda University
School of Behavioral Health
Department of Graduate Psychology

Education:
Ph.D. Clinical Psychology
Loma Linda University

M.A. in Clinical Psychology
Loma Linda University

Address:
UCLA Longevity Center
Peter V. Ueberroth Building
10945 Le Conte Avenue, Suite 3119
Los Angeles, CA 90095-6980
Phone (310) 206-2900
SWaleszonia@mednet.ucla.edu

Research and Professional Experience:

Inpatient and Outpatient neuropsychological assessment of the geriatric, adult, and child populations, in regard to neurological impairments, brain injury, and/or learning disabilities.

Examining the cognitive functioning in patients undergoing alcohol addiction treatment.

Name: Karen J. Miller, Ph.D.

Affiliation:

UCLA Longevity Center
David Geffen School of Medicine at UCLA
Semel Institute for Neuroscience & Human Behavior

Education:

PhD in Clinical Psychology
Fuller Seminary, School of Psychology

Address:

Peter V. Ueberroth Building
10945 Le Conte Avenue
Los Angeles, CA 90095-6980

Research and Professional Experience:

Early detection of cognitive decline, aging and memory, brain fitness

Professional Appointments:

Health Sciences Associate Clinical Professor of Psychiatry and Biobehavioral Sciences, Clinical Compensated Series, Step II, UCLA Semel Institute, Department of Psychiatry and Biobehavioral Sciences, Division of Geriatric Psychiatry

Honors:

2013 Exceptional Educator, Women in Leadership, National Academy of Neuropsychology

2012 American Psychological Association,
Division 40, Blue Ribbon Award for Research
2011 Outstanding Housestaff Teaching Award,
UCLA Medical School, Dept. of Psychiatry
2008 Semel Scholar Award, UCLA – Semel Institute
2007 Judith Braun Excellence in Research Award,
National Gero Nurses Association
2006 Outstanding Graduate Teaching Award,
UCLA Medical School, Department of Psychiatry

Publications Last Three Years:

1. Miller KJ, Siddarth P, Gaines JM, Parrish JM, Ercoli L, Marx K, Ronch J, Pilgram B, Burke K, Barczak N, Babcock B, Small GW. The Memory Fitness Study: Effects of a healthy aging intervention program on older adults. *American Journal of Geriatric Psychiatry* 2012 Jun;20(6):514-23. doi: 10.1097/JGP.0b013e318227f821.
2. Donix M, Burggren AC, Suthana NA, Siddarth P, Ekstrom AD, Krupa AK, Jones M, Martin-Harris L, Ercoli LM, Miller KJ, Small GW, Bookheimer SY. The influence of family history for Alzheimer's disease on hippocampal structure in healthy people. *American Journal of Geriatric Psychiatry* 2012;20(7):565-573.
3. Merrill DA, Siddarth P, Saito NY, Ercoli LM, Burggren AC, Kepe V, Lavretsky H, Miller KJ, Kim J, Huang SC, Bookheimer SY, Barrio JR, Small GW. Self-reported memory impairment and brain PET of amyloid and tau in middle-aged and older adults without dementia. *International Psychogeriatrics* 2012; Jul 24(7):1076-84.
4. Small GW, Siddarth P, Kepe V, Ercoli LM, Burggren AC, Bookheimer SY, Miller KJ, Kim J, Lavretsky H, Huang S-C, Barrio JR. Prediction of cognitive decline by positron emission tomography of brain amyloid and tau. *Archives of Neurology* 2012; 69:215-222.
5. Curiel AR, Miller KJ, Pollard K, Kim J, Kravitz J, Small GW. Anxiety and verbal memory performance in APOE-4 carriers and non-carriers ages 50 and above. *Aging Health* 2012; 8:99-104.
6. Ercoli LM, Small GW, Siddarth P, Kepe V, Huang S-C, Miller KJ, Lavretsky H, Bookheimer SY, Barrio J R, Silverman DHS. Assessment of dementia risk in aging adults using both FDG-PET and FDDNP-PET

imaging. *International Journal of Geriatric Psychiatry* 2012 Mar 1. doi: 10.1002/gps.2816. [Epub ahead of print].

7. Dye R, Miller KJ, Levine A, Singer E. Hormone Replacement Therapy and Risk for Neurogenerative Diseases. *International Journal of Alzheimer's Disease*, 2012; 1-18: doi:10.1155/2012/258454.
8. Lee GJ, Curiel AR, Miller KJ, Amano S, Gorsuch R, Small G W. (2012). Language performance in postmenopausal women with and without hormone therapy and men. *Aging Health* 2012; 8(6); 625-632.
9. Kaiser NC, Miller KJ, Siddarth P, Ercoli LM, Small GW. The impact of age and Alzheimer's disease risk factors on memory performance over time. *Aging Health.* 2013; 9(1):1-10.
10. Miller KJ, Dye RV, Kim J, Jennings JL, O'Toole E, Wong J, Siddarth P. The Effect of a Computerized Brain Exercise Program on Cognitive Performance in Older Adults. *American Journal of Geriatric Psychiatry.* 2013. Jul;21(7):655-63. doi: 10.1016/j.jagp.2013.01.077. Epub 2013 Apr 18.
11. Merrill DA, Siddarth P, Kepe V, Raja PV, Saito N, Ercoli LM, Miller KJ, Lavretsky H, Bookheimer SY, Barrio JR, Small GW. Vascular Risk and FDDNP-PET influence cognitive performance. *Journal of Alzheimer's Disease*. 2013:35;147-157.
12. Smid LM, Kepe V, Vinters HV, Bresjanac M, Toyokuni T, Satyamurthy N, Wong KP, Huang SC, Silverman DH, Miller K, Small GW, Barrio JR. Postmortem 3-D brain hemisphere cortical tau and amyloid-β pathology mapping and quantification as a validation method of neuropathology imaging. *Journal of Alzheimer's Disease*. 2013:336(2):261-74.
13. Chen ST, Siddarth P, Saito N, Rueda F, Haight T, Ercoli LM, Miller KJ, Lavretsky H, Barrio JR, Bookheimer SY, Small GW, Merrill D. Psychological well-being and regional brain amyloid and tau in mild cognitive impairment. *Am J Geriatr Psychiatry*. 2014; 22(4):362-9.
14. Bellone JA. and Miller KJ, Methods for improving neuroplasticity and memory functioning in the aging or compromised brain. *Long- and Short-Term Memory: Functions, Differences, and Effects of Injury (in press).*
15. Baerresen KM, Miller KJ, Hanson ER, Miller JS, Dye RV, Hartman RE, Vermeersch D, Small GW. Neuropsychological tests for predicting cognitive decline in older adults. *Journal of Neurodegenerative Disease Management (in press).*

In: Trait and State Anxiety
Editor: Abel Bradley
ISBN: 978-1-63484-840-4

Chapter 3

ATTENTION DEFICIT/HYPERACTIVITY DISORDER AND ANXIETY: IMPLICATIONS OF COMORBIDITY ON EXECUTIVE FUNCTION DEFICITS

Marisol Cueli[1,*], Paloma González-Castro[1], Trinidad García[1], Débora Areces[1], Stephen Loew[2] and Celestino Rodríguez[1]

[1]University of Oviedo, Spain
[2]University of New England, Australia

ABSTRACT

Attention Deficit with Hyperactivity Disorder (ADHD) is one of the most prevalent disorders in childhood and affects about 5% of school students. ADHD is characterized by three main symptoms: inattention, hyperactivity and impulsivity. These deficits suggest a problem in the voluntary control of behavior that is generally associated with executive functioning impairments (e.g., deficits in working memory, planning, organization, concentration, and cognitive flexibility). Moreover, ADHD is frequently accompanied by different disorders, especially anxiety,

[*] Corresponding author: Marisol Cueli. University of Oviedo. Department of Psychology. Plaza Feijoo s/n, 33003, Oviedo, Spain. Telephone. +34-985103255; Fax: +34-985104144. Email: cuelimarisol@uniovi.es.

which is present in 20% to 50% of ADHD cases. This comorbidity usually has important effects on the expression of ADHD deficits in both children and adolescents. Thus, it is necessary to systematically examine the potential consequences of this association. The primary goals of this study are to firstly carry out an exhaustive review of previous research on this topic, and thereafter analyze executive function profiles in a cohort of students with ADHD and anxiety (aged 6 to 16 years). In order to clearly describe the findings and results of these goals, the present chapter comprises the following structure: 1) A brief introduction describing ADHD and executive functions deficits, with a particular focus on comorbidity between ADHD and anxiety disorders; 2) The concept of anxiety and the different classifications of this disorder is discussed in relation to the most commonly-utilized assessment methods and instruments at the present time; 3) The implications of the presence of anxiety on executive deficits in ADHD are explained, and then examined in the light of an empirical study involving a small sample of students with these very characteristics (comorbid ADHD and anxiety disorders); 4) The results from this analysis are then discussed, and some practical implications are also presented. The aspects addressed in the present chapter will provide readers with an initial insight into this problematic aspect of ADHD, and its important consequences concerning children and adolescent individuals and their future academic achievement.

Keywords: anxiety, ADHD, executive function, comorbidity, child and adolescent ADHD

INTRODUCTION

Attention Deficit/Hyperactivity Disorder and Executive Function

According to the Diagnostic and Statistical Manual of Mental Disorders (DSM-5; American Psychiatric Association, 2013), Attention Deficit with Hyperactivity Disorder (ADHD) affects about 5% of students. With the publication of this new classification manual, ADHD is now categorized as a neurodevelopmental disorder. While there were no significant changes in terms of the main symptoms of the disorder with respect to previous classifications (inattention, hyperactivity and impulsivity), there are now three types of presentations (instead of subtypes) of ADHD: predominantly hyperactive/impulsive; predominantly inattentive; and combined presentation.. There have been a variety of studies aimed at analyzing different aspects of

ADHD, with many focusing on its etiology and comorbidity with other disorders.

Regarding etiology, ADHD is a heterogeneous disorder and is very unlikely to have a single cause, but rather, it is probably the result of a series of biological vulnerabilities interacting with other environmental variables, both psychosocial and biophysical (Herreros, Rubio, Sánchez and Gracia, 2002). According to Rommelse, Van der Stigchel and Sergeant (2008) however, given that the impulsivity and attention deficit are associated with deficits in the voluntary control of behavior, these ADHD deficits have been related to neurologic disorders in fronto-striatal circuits, which are areas of special relevance in executive functioning (Carboni-Román, del Río Grande, Capilla, Maestú and Ortiz, 2006; Epstein et al., 2007).

In this sense, different studies have indicated that children with ADHD have problems in a variety of tasks related to executive control, mainly in response inhibition, working memory, cognitive flexibility and planning (Barkley, 1998; Willcutt, Sonuga-Barke, Nigg and Sergeant, 2008; García, González-Pienda et al., 2014). Moreover, these deficits also explain some of the difficulties present in children and adolescents with ADHD in both academic and social contexts.

Furthermore, another important aspect to mention in relation to ADHD is its comorbidity with other disorders (Sciberras et al., 2014). These can be both externalized, such as disruptive behavior disorders (Hummer et al., 2011), and internalized, such as anxiety or depression (González-Castro, Rodríguez, Cueli, García and Álvarez-García, 2015). Beyond gender (girls are more inattentive than boys), or age (hyperactivity and impulsivity tend to decrease with the age), the presence of these associated disorders can affect the symptoms displayed, and thus the treatment and prognosis of the ADHD.

ADHD and Comorbidity with Anxiety Disorders

Some researchers emphasize the importance of identifying comorbidity in ADHD cases, as it is an essential determining factor in the course of the disorder (Bloemsma et al., 2013; Humphreys, Aguirre and Lee, 2012; Rodríguez, González-Castro, García, Núñez and Álvarez, 2014). Comorbidity has been reported to be associated with different disorders, such as learning difficulties, depression, oppositional defiant disorder, behavior disorders, as well as anxiety and mood disorders (González-Castro et al., 2014; Skirbekk, Hansen, Oerbeck and Kristensen, 2011). Regarding anxiety, comorbidity with

ADHD is estimated at 20-25% (Bloemsma et al., 2013). The diverse estimates of the studies may be due to the extensive overlap of symptoms in these syndromes (ADHD and anxiety), so it may be difficult to determine whether a child has developed hyperactivity and inattention because of anxiety, or whether low self-esteem derived from ADHD has caused the anxious behavior. Anxious children usually display a permanent state of worry or apprehension that is difficult to control (Bloemsma et al., 2013). This can be confused with some typical symptoms of ADHD, such as restlessness, fatigue, difficulty concentrating, irritability, muscle tension, and sleep disturbance. In short, there is a strong association between ADHD and internalizing disorders (Ferrin & Vance, 2014), which highlights the importance of researching not only the symptomatology, but also the association between the two disorders.

Anxiety: Classifications and Assessment

Following to Gümüs, Cakin-Memik and Agaoglu (2015), anxiety is understood to be a protective and adaptive emotion that could be defined as 'restlessness accompanied by expectation of danger,' which might vary depending on previous life experiences. According to the DSM-5 (American Psychiatric Association, 2013), anxiety disorders could be classified into the following different categories: Separation Anxiety Disorder; Selective Mutism; Specific Phobia; Social Anxiety Disorder; Panic Disorder; Panic Attack; Agoraphobia; and Generalized Anxiety Disorder.

Generalized anxiety disorder (GAD) is one of the most common anxiety conditions that co-occurs with ADHD in childhood and adolescence, with estimates indicating that these disorders co-occur in up to 15% of youth (Elia, Arcos-Burgos, Bolton, Ambrosini, Berrettini and Muenke, 2009; Elkins, Carpener, Pincus and Comer, 2014).). It is characterized by uncontrollable and interfering worry and related symptoms, and associated with considerable impairments in its own right (Mogg et al., 2015). Meta-analytical work by Willcutt et al. (2012) demonstrates that, compared to healthy controls, children and adolescents with ADHD-Combined Subtype (ADHD-C) are 6.5 times more likely to meet criteria for comorbid GAD.

Other classifications, are related to the *reference theory*, in which is necessary to differentiate between the *interactive theory* and the *behavioral theory* (Martínez-Algeciras & Rodríguez-Jiménez, 2013). The interactive theory appears to be in line with an earlier theory proposed by Spielberger, Gorsuch, Lushene, Vagg and Jacobs (1983), in which anxiety can be either 'trait' or 'state' derived. These authors differentiated between trait anxiety, as a personality dimension, and state anxiety, as a transient mood state. Trait anxiety refers to a general level of stress that characterizes certain individuals that are often easily stressed and anxious, while state anxiety is characterized as a state of heightened emotions that appears in response to danger or fear of a particular situation.

In contrast, the behavioral theory has referred to the anxiety as a construct that brings together a set of motor, cognitive and psychophysiological responses elicited by certain background variables, such as environmental stimuli and the responses of the subject (Méndez & Macia, 1994), setting in motion a triple-response system. In this system, the most common motor responses are: trembling voice and limbs, psychophysiological responses, cardiovascular changes and elevated blood pressure, followed by cognitive responses to the presence of thoughts and images that negatively evaluate situations, anticipating unfavorable responses (Méndez & Macia, 1994).

According to the above perspectives, anxiety can be viewed as a reaction or emotional response that includes multiple expressions. Taking into account these perspectives, two types of assessment methodologies should be considered. First, those based on questionnaires filled out by the subject, such as the STAI-C (Spielberger, Goursch and Lushene, 1990), which assess state and trait anxiety in children between 9 and 15 years old; or the Inventory of Anxiety Situations and Responses (ISRA; Cano & Miguel, 2002), which assess cognitive, motor and physiological anxiety in children older than 16 years. Second, those based on measures aimed at assessing the subject's psycho-physiological responses to the anxiety, such as heart rate or the psychogalvanic skin response. In this second group of methodologies there are useful instruments for obtaining less subjective data, such as the Galvanic Skin Resistance (GSR). The GSR is a well-accepted and validated marker of physiologic activation (Katsis, Katertsidis and Fotiadis, 2011; Sequeira, Hot, Silvert and Delplanque, 2009). It assesses the conductance of the skin o psychogalvanic skin response. Skin is an organ of three layers (epidermis, dermis and subdermis). In the subdermis (mainly in the palms of the hands), are the sweat glands. These glands act as electric resistances so that when filled with sweat, its resistance decreases (conductivity increases). Activation of these sweat glands depends of Autonomic Nervous System (ANS) which responds to thoughts, emotions and motivations. Thus, authors as Picard, Vyzas and Healy (2001) accomplished 81% accuracy for the detection of anger, hate, grief, platonic love, romantic love, joy, reverence and the neutral state, based on the utilization of statistical methods and features calculated from the respiration, skin conductance, blood volume pulse, and electromyogram of a single individual.

In any case, independently of the classification or the type of assessment, the presence of these kinds of anxiety has been identified as a determinant in the executive function of the subject (Sadeh & Bredemier, 2011; Schatz & Rostain, 2006; Sørensen, Plessen, Nicholasn and Lundervold, 2010). Taking this into account, some studies have now been focused on the influence of anxiety over the performance or execution of a task, mainly, in students who present with ADHD and anxiety.

Implications of ADHD and Anxiety Comorbidity in Executive Functioning

As mentioned before, most current estimates of the incidence of comorbidity between ADHD and anxiety range between disturbingly high rates. This is especially relevant given that the consequences of the association could be an effect in various situations, including scholastic, familiar and social contexts, with more difficulties concerning adaptation and less social competence (Bowen, Chavira, Bailey, Stein and Stein, 2008).

Furthermore, the presence of anxiety could modulate the typical clinical expression of ADHD, by causing a decrease in impulsivity and an increase of attentional deficit in children with ADHD and anxiety (Bowen et al., 2008; Brown, 2000; Schatz & Rostain, 2006). Also, the presence of anxiety could have an effect on the executive function of children and adolescents with ADHD that is associated with major difficulties in the performance of tasks, particularly those tasks that include working memory, planning, cognitive flexibility and information processing (Barkley, 2006; Schatz and Rostain, 2006; Derakshan & Eysenck, 2009; Sørensen et al., 2010).

This influence of anxiety on executive function is also interpretable within the contexts of the *processing efficiency theory* (Eysenck & Calvo, 1992) and the *attentional control theory* (Eysenck, Derackman, Santos and Calvo, 2007). According to Wilson (2008), the central tenet of processing efficiency theory is, that as well as pre-empting resources in working memory, increased anxiety provides a motivational function that leads to the allocation of additional effort in an attempt to maintain task performance. On the other hand, the attentional control theory purports that anxiety reduces attentional control by increasing the influence of the stimulus-driven attentional system at the cost of goal directed control.

In this sense, the study conducted by Sørensen et al. (2010) is one of the most outstanding and recent references to date. These authors investigated the impact of the coexistence of anxiety on the ability to regulate behavior in a sample of children with ADHD, using a measure of executive functions known as the BRIEF scale, in its version designed for families (Gioia, Isquith, Guy and Kenworthy, 2000). This study involves four groups of children (ADHD, Anxiety, Anxiety+ADHD, and Controls), which were compared in the different measures provided by the scale. In this study, children with ADHD and comorbid anxiety showed significantly greater difficulties in response inhibition than the other three groups. Furthermore, in the group with anxiety-only, some difficulties in inhibition, emotional control, working memory and cognitive flexibility (expected in principle only in the ADHD sample) were also found. These results indicated that the ability to regulate one´s behavior in children with ADHD may be exacerbated by the presence of symptoms of anxiety. On the other hand, and in the context of using performance measures, the study conducted by Lundervold et al. (2011) is also worth noting. They examined whether adults with ADHD performed differently to controls on various measures of accuracy, variability and vigilance, and whether these differences were related to the presence of affective fluctuations (similar to those found in anxiety disorders). Results indicated that adults with ADHD showed impairments on the different measures of executive functions. In addition, within the ADHD group, those who reported affective fluctuations were found to be slower and more prone to be distracted by conflicting stimuli than the group without such fluctuations. The results suggest the presence of different patterns of attentional problems as a function of the co-occurrence of affective symptoms.

In the same way, the presence of which one of two distinctive forms of anxiety (trait versus state anxiety) may also be a determining factor for differential performance on executive function tasks. For this specific reason, Sadeh and Bredemier (2011) analyzed the effect of trait anxiety on subjects' attention and susceptibility to distractibility, using a sample of 68 college students. Their results showed that an increase in trait anxiety was related to poor performance on selective attention tasks, defined as the ability to select the relevant stimulus stream, suppress the irrelevant streams, and maintain attention on the relevant information (Lackner et al., 2013). This was also the case in a study conducted by Rodríguez, González-Castro, García, Núñez and Álvarez (2014), with a sample of 220 students aged 8 to 12. On this occasion, however, no differences were found (neither in selective nor sustained attention) between children with ADHD-only and ADHD+Trait Anxiety.

These results are in agreement with those obtained by Vloet, Konrad, Herpetz-Dahlmann, Polier and Günter, (2010), who examined impulsivity, set-shifting and different parameters of attention (alertness, sustained and divided attention) in a sample of students with ADHD, anxiety and controls, using various computerized attention tests. Consistent with other previous studies (Hammerness et al., 2010; Korenblum, Chen, Manassis and Schachar, 2007), these authors found no effect of anxiety on impulsive behavior and/or attention in ADHD.

In this context, and given the lack of agreement in previous research, one of the objectives of this study was to analyze the effect of anxiety on executive functioning in a sample of students with ADHD and different levels of anxiety (without anxiety, medium level of anxiety, and high level of anxiety). The BRIEF scale (Gioia et al., 2000) administered to families was used to assess eight main executive function components. According to the study conducted by Sørensen et al. (2010), who used the same assessment instrument, significant differences in the various components of executive function can be expected to be found among such groups, as those with higher levels of anxiety are more prone to show executive impairments than are other students.

METHODS

Participants

A sample of 41 children with ADHD took part in this study, 33 (80.5%) male and 8 (19.5%) female. Their ages ranged between 6 and 16 years (M = 10.39; SD = 3.183). All participants had an IQ higher than 80 according to their results in the Weschler Intelligence Scale for Children-Fourth Edition (WISC-IV; Weschler, 2005) (M = 96; SD = 8.363).

Participants were assigned to following three groups as a function of the presence of anxiety symptomatology. Two different measures of anxiety were used for this purpose: The STAIC method (measuring trait and state anxiety); and the GSR method (measuring psycho-physiological anxiety).

Group 1 (without anxiety) was composed of 12 children with a mean of age of 9.82 (SD = 3.314) and mean IQ of 96.50 (SD = 8.017). Students in this group did not show any evidence of anxiety in either of the measures referred to above.

Group 2 (medium anxiety) was made up with 21 children with a mean of age of 10.81 years (*SD* =3.248) and mean IQ of 95.76 (*SD* = 9.011). These students showed anxiety symptoms in only one assessment instrument.

Group 3 (high anxiety) was comprised by 7 children with a mean of age of 12.20 (*SD* = 2.786) and mean IQ of 96.00 (*SD* = 8.000). These students showed anxiety symptoms in both measures.

There were no statistically significant between-group differences in IQ or age. All participants were attending public and state schools in Asturias (Spain), and none were receiving pharmacological treatment.

Inclusion Criteria

The subjects with ADHD were identified at the Child and Adolescent Psychiatric Service of the Central University Hospital of Asturias, according to the *Diagnostic and Statistical Manual of Mental Disorders-IV, text revision* (DSM-IV-TR; American Psychiatry Association, 2002). This diagnostic method was verified by examiners using additional measures, based on performance (Test of Variables of Attention -TOVA- which is a continuous performance test; Greenberg, 1996), and the assessment of ADHD symptoms by means of the Diagnostic Interview Schedule for Children (DISC-IV; Shaffer, Fisher, Lucas, Dulcan and Schwab-Stone, 2000). Test-retest reliability reported for the Spanish version of the DISC-IV was “fair to moderate agreement” (kappas from .48 to .59) (Bravo et al., 2001).

Instruments

Two different instruments were used to evaluate anxiety and assign students to the different diagnostic groups, while the assessment of executive functions was made through the administration of the BRIEF scale (Gioia et al., 2000) to families.

Anxiety Measures

State-Trait Anxiety Inventory for Children (STAI-C; Spielberger et al., 1990). This instrument consists of two 20-item scales that measure state and trait anxiety in children. The state anxiety scale examines short-term anxiety, which is usually situation-specific. It prompts the child to rate 20 statements on a 3-point scale ranging from ‘*Hardly ever true*’ to ‘*Often true.*’ The trait anxiety scale measures long-term anxiety (or how the child generally feels). Interpretation of the information provided by STAI-C is based upon higher scores corresponding to higher levels of anxiety. Variables taken into consideration included state anxiety (raw scores and percentiles) and trait anxiety (raw scores and percentiles). Spielberger et al. (1983) reported alpha coefficients of .90 to .93 for internal consistency and .73 to .86 for test-retest reliability. The scale has demonstrated convergent validity by having statistically significant correlations with other anxiety scales. Alpha coefficients in the present study were adequate, with values of .86 to .89 for trait and state anxiety scales, respectively. A percentile 70 or higher in this test is associated with high anxiety.

The Galvanic Skin Resistance (GSR). It is a biofeedback system that allows the observation and modification of physiological signals of tension and stress. The GSR can detect and amplify signals of resistance or galvanic skin response. Galvanic response reflects variations in the sweat gland skin pore size (both responses are controlled by the sympathetic nervous system). The skin resistance increases when the subject is calm and relaxed, and decreases when the subject is under a state of stress or tension. In order to get a measure of this response, the index and middle fingers have to be placed on the sensing plaques incorporated in the device. Either hand can be used.

The GSR system includes a data-recorder which shows the changes in temperature and skin resistance. Before taking the measure of interest, a baseline needs to be recorded. One minute is enough to establish the baseline. Once the baseline is entered, subjects are asked to perform a relatively demanding cognitive task (e.g., counting numbers backward 'by three-s'), and measurements are taken again during task performance. Finally, another minute is allowed to evaluate the final stress-activation level and the time required to return to the baseline state. Three different profiles can be identified using this test:

- Anxious Profile: activation increases to above the baseline, continues at that level during the task, and does not decrease after task completion.
- Unmotivated Profile: activation stays low, or at the baseline, continues in that position during the task, and remains the same after the task.
- Standard Profile: activation is initially low, or at the baseline, goes up during the task, and goes down once the task is completed.

The presence of an anxious profile was used as a criterion to determine the presence of psychophysiological indicators of anxiety.

Executive Functions

The BRIEF scale (Behavior Rating Inventory of Executive Function; Gioia et al., 2000) was used for this purpose. There are different versions of this questionnaire. The most frequently employed is based on information provided by the family. It is applicable from ages 5 to 18 years and it assesses the frequency with which children and adolescents display certain problematic behaviors related to deficits in executive functions at home and/or in school. For this purpose, it uses a Likert-type response format ranging from 1 to 3, where 1 is never, 2 is sometimes, and 3 is often. The scale is made up of 86 items (72 computable items and 14 additional ones). The latter do not contribute to the score but are useful to adjust possible interventions. The remaining 72 items form 8 scales: Inhibit, Shift, Emotional Control, Initiate, Working Memory, Plan/Organize, Organization of Materials, and Monitor, which in turn are grouped into two main indexes: the Behavioral Regulation Index (BRI), made up of the first three scales, and the Metacognition Index (MI), made up of the remaining five. Both indexes form the Global Executive Composite (GEC) score. High scores in these scales and indices indicate executive functions deficit. This instrument has shown its utility for the assessment of executive functions in a broad range of clinical conditions, especially in ADHD (García, González-Pienda et al., 2014; McCandless & O'Laughlin, 2007; Toplak et al., 2009). The alpha coefficients range from.94 to .82 for the different components of the scale.

Procedure

After reviewing the results in the measures of anxiety, children were assigned to the correspondence group as a function of the presence or absence of anxiety in both STAIC and GSR. The following groups were created: without anxiety (without symptomatology in STAIC nor GSR), medium anxiety (with symptomatology in one of the instruments), and high anxiety (symptoms in both types of measurement). Students completed the STAIC questionnaire and were administered GSR measures, while parents were asked to score the frequency with which their children showed different problematic behaviors related to executive function deficits, by means of the BRIEF scale. Students volunteered for the study, and all provided signed parental-consent.

Design and Data Analysis

An ex-post-facto comparative-descriptive design with three groups was used. Once the normality of the variables was tested, data were analyzed using multivariate analysis of covariance (MANCOVA). The dependent variables were group scores in the eight components of the BRIEF scale, and its indices (BRI, MI, and GEC). IQ and age were included as covariates. We used the value of Wilks' lambda to determine possible significant differences in all the dependent variables taken conjointly. In those cases where Wilks' lambda was significant ($p < .05$), the results of the univariate analyses of the variance (ANOVAs) were interpreted. For observed statistically significant differences among groups, data from effect size and post-hoc analyses were provided. Effect size interpretation followed Cohen's (1988) criteria, which establish that the effect is small when $\eta p^2 = .01$ ($d = .20$), medium when $\eta p^2 = .059$ ($d = .50$), and high when $\eta p^2 = .138$ ($d = .80$). Scheffé's post-hoc analyses were carried out to examine differences between pairs of groups. All data were analyzed by means of SPSS vs. 19.

Results

Table 1 shows the means and standard deviations of each group for all dependent variables. As can be observed, means (and levels of executive function deficits) increase as functions of the levels of anxiety, with the 'ADHD and high anxiety' group showing the highest scores in the different components of the BRIEF scale. This is particularly visible in the cases of the main indexes (BRI, MI and GEC). Despite these observable differences however, MANCOVA showed no statistically significant differences among groups in this set of variables ($p = .08$). None of the covariates (age and IQ) reached statistical significance ($p = .123$ and $p = .345$, respectively).

When considering the means of the different groups together, results show that Working Memory and Plan/Organize are the components in which students have more deficits, with Organization of the Materials being the least problematic area in this sense.

Table 1. Means (M) and Standard Deviations (SD) for each diagnostic group

	Group 1 (*n* = 12)		Group 2 (*n* = 21)		Group 3 (*n* = 7)	
	M	*SD*	*M*	*SD*	*M*	*SD*
Inhibit	15.75	4.495	18.33	4.564	18.57	5.798
Shift	16.50	3.754	17.00	3.987	17.00	3.873
Emotional Control	13.92	5.017	17.10	5.412	18.29	6.102
Initiate	15.17	2.209	15.19	2.750	16.43	2.878
Working Memory	22.25	4.181	22.05	3.943	23.43	4.315
Plan/Organize	22.35	4.004	24.00	5.222	28.14	3.579
Organization of Materials	12.50	4.681	13.81	3.296	12.43	3.645
Monitor	16.67	3.085	16.67	3.085	17.95	3.514
BRI	46.17	11.384	52.43	12.011	53.86	13.184
MI	90.58	15.957	96.24	15.456	99.86	9.651
Global (GEC)	136.75	22.357	148.67	24.518	153.71	15.639

Note: Group 1= ADHD without anxiety; Group 2= ADHD + medium levels of anxiety; Group 3= ADHD + high levels of anxiety. High scores in these components are indicative of deficit.

Discussion and Conclusion

The main goals of this study were to make an exhaustive review of previous research on this topic, and to analyze the executive functions profile of a group of students with ADHD and anxiety (ages 6 to 16 years). In order to reach these goals, in the first part of the chapter we presented a review of theories and studies focused on ADHD and anxiety. We could conclude that there are different theories aimed at explaining anxiety and ADHD, and that they are linked to different methods designed to assess this symptomatology (i.e., questionnaires and physiological measures). Also, the previous studies have shown an association between ADHD and anxiety and its affects in different contexts (such as the scholar, familiar and social contexts). Also, it has an impact on executive functions in subjects that are reflected in previous research as increased attention deficits and decreased impulsivity tendencies. To more deeply explore this issue, we also carried out an experimental investigation, the results of which are presented and discussed in the second part of this chapter.

Thus, in the second part of the chapter, the aim was to analyze the effect of anxiety on executive functioning in a sample of students with ADHD and different levels of anxiety. The BRIEF scale (Gioia et al., 2000) administered to families was used to assess eight main executive function components. The results showed that, although the different groups (i.e., without anxiety, medium level of anxiety, and high level of anxiety) were found to have executive profiles that were quite similar, there was a tendency to find higher deficits in the BRIEF scales and indices as the level of anxiety increases. This may be partially explained by the small sample size used, and the presence of unbalanced groups. Nevertheless, these results initially suggest that the presence of symptoms of anxiety (and the intensity of these symptoms) may modify the expression of the executive functioning deficits that characterize ADHD. This finding is coherent with previous studies, which have utilized both observation and/or performance measures (Lundervold et al., 2011; Sadeh & Bredemier, 2011; Sørensen et al., 2010).

Results also showed that the general sample had special problems in the components of working memory and organization. Thus, students with ADHD in the present study, regardless the level of anxiety they present, showed difficulties related to problem solving, information processing and organization, and the performance of tasks that require a series of steps sequenced properly. This is consistent with the characterization of ADHD as an executive functions disorder (Barkley, 1998; García, González-Pienda et al., 2014; Navarro, 2009; Willcutt et al., 2008). However, and given the core symptoms of the disorder (i.e., hyperactivity/impulsivity and deficits in attention), some difficulties in areas related to the first group of symptoms (mainly in response inhibition) would not be unexpected. The lack of a specific deficit in this study may be related to the composition of the sample itself. Specifically, it could be related to a major proportion of students presenting with the inattentive form of the disorder. The relationship between organization and planning deficits and this form of ADHD-presentation has been highlighted in previous research, using the BRIEF scale (García, González-Castro et al., 2014; Navarro-González and García-Villamisar, 2011). This is an aspect that should be controlled for in any future studies in this area.

Finally, we can generally conclude that the relationship between anxiety and ADHD is an important association that needs to be considered during the diagnostic procedures of both disorders. Detection of the former could be an opportunity to carry out interventions aimed at reducing anxiety symptoms, which in turn, can increase some of the main deficits in ADHD. Furthermore, measures of psychological aspects related to anxiety should be included in the assessment protocols, given that these are best able to detect increased anxiety levels and that not all students exhibit the presence of anxiety in questionnaires.

REFERENCES

American Psychiatric Association. (2002). *Diagnostic and Statistical Manual of Mental Disorders. (4th Edition, rev.).* Washigton DC: Author.

American Psychiatric Association. (2013). *Diagnostic and statistical manual of mental disorders (5th ed.).* Washington, DC: Author.

Barkley, R. A. (1998). *Attention Deficit Hyperactivity Disorder. A Handbook for Diagnosis and Treatment.* New York: Guilford Press.

Barkley, R. A. (2006). *Attention-deficit hyperactivity disorder: A handbook for diagnosis and treatment (3rd ed.).* New York: Guilford Press.

Bloemsma, J. M., Boer, F., Arnold, R., Banaschewski, T., Faraone, S. V., Buitelaar, J. K., Sergeant, J. A., Rommelse, N. and Oosterlaan, J. (2013). Comorbid anxiety and neurocognitive dysfunctions in children with ADHD. *European Child & Adolescent Psychiatry, 22*(4), 225-234.

Bravo, M., Ribera, J., Rubio-Stipec, M. R., Canino, G., Shrout, P., Ramírez, R., Fábregras, L., Chavez, L., Alegría, M., Bauermeister, J. J. and Taboas, A. M. (2001). Test-Retest Reliability of the spanish version of the Diagnostic Interview Schedule for Children (DISC-IV). *Journal of Abnormal Child Psychology, 29*(5), 433-444.

Bowen, R., Chavira, D. A., Bailey, K., Stein, M. T. and Stein, M. B. (2008). Nature of anxiety comorbid with attention deficit hyperactivity disorder in children from a pediatric primary care setting. *Psychiatry Research, 157*(1-3), 201-209.

Brown, T. E. (2000). *Attention-deficit disorders and comorbidities in children adolescents, and adults.* Washington, DC: American PsychiatricPress.

Cano, A. and Miguel, J. (2002). *Inventario de situaciones y respuestas de ansiedad ISRA manual. (5ª. Ed.).* Madrid: TEA.

Carboni-Román, A., del Río Grande, D., Capilla, A., Maestú, F. and Ortiz, T. (2006). Bases neurobiológicas de las dificultades de aprendizaje. *Revista de Neurología, 42*, 171-175.

Cohen, J. (1988). *Statistical power analysis for the behavioral sciences* (2nd ed.). Hillsdale, NJ: Erlbaum.

Derakshan, N. and Eysenck, M. W. (2009). Anxiety, Processing Efficiency, and Cognitive Performance. New Developments from Attentional Control Theory. *European Psychologist*, *14*(2), 168–176. doi: 10.1027/1016-9040.14.2.168.

Elia, J., Arcos-Burgos, M., Bolton, L. K., Ambrosini, J. P., Berrettini, W. and Muenke, M. (2009). ADHD latent class clusters: DSM-IV subtypes and comorbidity. *Psychiatry Research*, *170*, 192–198.

Elkins, R. M., Carpener, A. L., Pincus, D. B. and Comer, J. S. (2014). Inattention symptoms and the diagnosis of comorbid attention-deficit/hyperactivity disorder among youth with generalized anxiety disorder. *Journal of Anxiety Disorders*, *28*, 754-760. http://dx.doi.org/10.1016/j.janxdis.2014.09.003.

Epstein, J. N., Casey, B. J., Tonev, S. T., Davidson, M. C., Reiss, A. L., Garrett, A., Hinshaw, S. P., Greenhill, L. L., Glover, G., Shafritz, K. M., Vitolo, A., Kotler, L. A., Jarrett, M. A. and Spicer, J. (2007). ADHD and medication related brain activation effects in concordantly affected parent-child dyads with ADHD. *Journal of Child Psychology and Psychiatry*, *48*(9), 899-913. doi: 10.1111/j.1469-7610.2007.01761.x.

Eysenck, M. W. and Calvo, M. G. (1992). Anxiety and performance: The processing efficiency theory. *Cognition and Emotion*, *6*, 409–434.

Eysenck, M. W., Derakshan, N., Santos, R. and Calvo, M. G. (2007). Anxiety and cognitive performance: Attentional control theory. *Emotion*, *7*, 336–353.

Ferrin, M. and Vance, A. (2014). Differential effects of anxiety and depressive symptoms on working memory components in children and adolescents with ADHD combined type and ADHD inattentive type. *European Child and Adolescent Psychiatry*, *23*, 1161-1173. doi: 10.1007/s00787-013-0509-4.

García, T., González-Castro, P., Rodríguez, C., Cueli, M., Álvarez-García, D. and Álvarez, L. (2014). Executive function alterations in attention deficit/hyperactivity disorder subtypes. *Psicología Educativa*, *20*(1), 23-32. doi:10.1016/j.pse.2014.05.003.

García. T., González-Pienda, J. A., Rodríguez; C., Álvarez, D. and Álvarez, L. (2014). Psychometric characteristics of the BRIEF scale for the assessment of executive functions in Spanish clinical population. *Psicothema*, *26* (1), 47-54.

Gioia, G. A., Isquith, P. K., Guy, S. and Kenworthy, L. (2000). *BRIEF: Behavior Rating Inventory of Executive Function professional manual.* Lutz, FL: PsychologicalAssessmentResources.

González-Castro, P., Álvarez, L., Núñez, J. C., González-Pienda, J.A., Álvarez, D. and Muñiz, J. (2010). Cortical activation y attentional control in ADAH subtypes. *International Journal of Clinical & Health Psychology*, *10* (1), 23 – 39.

Greenberg, M. L. (1996). *Test of Variables of Attention (TOVA-TOVA-A)*. Los Alamitos, CA: U.A.D.

Gümüs, Y. Y., Çakin-Memik, N. and Agaoglu, B. (2015). Anxiety disorders comorbidity in children and adolescents with attention deficit hyperactivity disorder. *Archives of Neuropsychiatry*, *52*, 185-193. doi: 10. 5152/npa.2015.7024.

Hammerness, P., Geller, D., Petty, C., Lamb, A., Bristol, E. and Biederman, J. (2010). Does ADHD moderate the manifestation of anxiety disorders in children? *European Child and Adolescent Psychiatry*, *19*(2), 107-112.

Herreros, O., Rubio, B., Sánchez, F. and Gracia, R. (2002). Etiology of Attention Deficit Hyperactivity Disorder: a review. *Revista de Psiquiatría Infantojuvenil*, *19*(1), 82-88.

Hummer, T. A., William, G., Kronenberger, W. G., Wang, Y., Dunn, D. W., Mosier, K. M., kalnin, A. J. and Mathews, V. P. (2011). Executive Functioning Characteristics Associated with ADHD Comorbidity in Adolescents with Disruptive Behavior Disorders. *Journal of Abnormal Child Psychology*, *39*(1), 11-19.

Humphreys, K. L., Aguirre, V. P. and Lee, S. S. (2012). Association of anxiety and ODD/CD in children with and without ADHD. *Journal of Clinical Child and Adolescent Psychology*, *41*(3), 370-377.

Katsis, C. D., Katertsidis, N. S. and Fotiadis, D. I. (2011). An integrated system based on physiological signals for the assessment of affective states in patients with anxiety disorders. *Biomedical Signal Processing and Control*, *6*(3), 261-268. doi:10.1016/j.bspc.2010.12.001.

Korenblum, C. B., Chen, S. X., Manassis, K. and Schachar, R. J. (2007). Performance monitoring and response inhibition in anxiety disorders with and without comorbid ADHD. *Depression and Anxiety*, *24*, 227-232.

Lackner, C. L., Santesso, D. L., Dywan, J., Wade, T. J. and Segalowitz, S. J. (2013). Electrocortical indices of selective attention predict adolescent executive functioning. *Biological Psychology*, *93*(2), 325-333.

Lundervold, A. J., Adolfsdottir, S., Halleland, H., Halmøy, A., Plessen, K. and Haavik, J. (2011). Attention Network Test in adults with ADHD-the impact of affective fluctuations. *Behavioral and Brain Functions*, *27*, 7-27. doi: 10.1186/1744-9081-7-27.

Martínez-Algeciras, K. A. and Rodríguez-Jiménez, O. R. (2013). Exploratory analysis of validity of the Inventory of Anxiety Situations and Responses (ISRA) adapted. *Acta Colombiana de Psicología*, *16*(1), 57-66.

McCandless, S. and O'Laughlin, L. (2007). The Clinical Utility of the Behavior Rating Inventory of Executive Function (BRIEF) in the Diagnosis of ADHD. *Journal of Attention Disorders*, *10*(4), 381-389. doi: 10.1177/108 7054706292115.

Méndez, F. and Macia, D. (1994). Evaluación de los problemas de ansiedad. En R. Fernández (Ed.), *Evaluación Conductual Hoy: Un enfoque para el cambio en psicología clínica y de la salud.*, (pp. 426-460). Madrid: Pirámide.

Mogg K., Salum, G. A., Bradley, B. P., Gadelha, A., Pan, P., Alvarenga, P., Rohde, L. A., Pine, D. S. and Manfro, G. G. (2015). Attention network functioning in children with anxiety disorders, attention-deficit/hyperactivity disorder and non-clinical anxiety. *Psychological Medicine*, *45*(12), 2633-2646. doi: 10.1017/S0033291715000586.

Navarro, M. I. (2009). Procesos cognitivos y ejecutivos en niños con Trastorno por Déficit de Atención con Hiperactividad, una investigación empírica. Tesis doctoral inédita.

Navarro-González, M. I. and García-Villamisar, D. A. (2011). Executive functioning in Attention Deficit Hyperactivity Disorder: an ecologic perspective of the differnt profiles between inattentive and combined subtypes. *Revista de Psicopatología y Psicología Clínica*, *16*,113-124.

Picard, R. W., Vyzas, E. and Healy, J. (2001). Toward machine emotional intelligence: analysis of affective physiological state. *IEEE Transactions on Pattern Analysis Machine Intelligence*, *23*(10), 1175–1191.

Rodríguez, C., González-Castro, P., García, T., Núñez, J. C. and Álvarez, L. (2014). Attentional functions and trait anxiety in children with ADHD. *Learning and Individual Differences*, *35*, 147-152.doi: 10.1016/j.lindif. 2014.07.010.

Rommelse, N. N. J., Van der Stigchel, S. and Sergeant, J. A. (2008). A review on eye movement studies in childhood and adolescent psychiatry. *Brain and Cognition*, *68*, 391-414. doi: 10.1016/j.bandc.2008.08.025.

Sadeh, N. and Bredemeier, K. (2011). Individual differences at high perceptual load: the relation between trait anxiety and selective attention. *Cognition and Emotion*, *25*(4), 747-55. doi: 10.1080/02699931.2010.500566.

Sciberras, E., Lycett, K., Efron, D., Mensah, F., Gerner, B. and Hiscock, H. (2014). Anxiety in children with Attention-Deficit/Hyperactivity Disorder. *Pediatrics*, *133*(5), 801-808.

Schatz, D. B. and Rostain, A. L. (2006). ADHD With Comorbid Anxiety A Review of the Current Literature *Journal of Attention Disorders*, *10*, 141-150.

Shaffer, D., Fisher, P., Lucas, C. P., Dulcan, M. K. and Schwab-Stone, M. E. (2000). Diagnostic interview schedule for children version IV (NIMH DISC-IV): Description, differences from previous versions and reliability of some common diagnoses. *Journal of the American Academy of Child and Adolescent Psychiatry*, *39*(1), 28-38.

Sequeira, H., Hot, P., Silvert, L. and Delplanque, S. (2009). Electrical autonomic correlates of emotion. *International Journal of Psychophysiology*, *71* (1), 50–56. doi: 10.1016/j.ijpsycho.2008.07.009.

Shaffer, D., Fisher, P., Lucas, C. P., Dulcan, M. K. and Schwab-Stone, M. E. (2000). Diagnostic interview schedule for children version IV (NIMH DISC-IV): Description, differences from previous versions and reliability of some common diagnoses. *Journal of the American Academy of Child and Adolescent Psychiatry*, *39*(1), 28-38. doi: http://dx.doi.org/10.1097/00004583-200001000-00014.

Skirbekk, B., Hansen, B. H., Oerbeck, B. and Kristensen, H. (2011). The relationship between sluggish cognitive tempo, subtypes of attention-deficit/hyperactivity disorder, and anxiety disorders. *Journal of Abnormal Child Psychology*, *39*(4), 513-525.

Sørensen, L., Plessen, K. J., Nicholas, J. and Lundervold, A. J. (2011). Is behavioral regulation in children with ADHD aggravated by comorbid anxiety disorder? *Journal of Attention Disorders*, *15*(1), 56-66. doi: 10.1177/1087054709356931.

Spielberger, C. D., Gorsuch, R. L., Lushene, R., Vagg, P. R. and Jacobs, G. A. (1983). *Manual for the State-Trait Anxiety Inventory*. Palo Alto, CA: Consulting Psychologists Press. [Spanish version: *STAI*. Madrid. TEA Editions, 1990].

Spielberger, C. D., Goursch, R. L. and Lushene, R. E. (1990). *State-Trait Anxiety Inventory for Children-Parent Form.*, STAI. Madrid. TEA Ediciones.

Toplak, M. E., Bucciarelli, S. M., Jain, U. and Tannock, R. (2009). Executive Functions: Performance-Based Measures and the Behavior Rating Inventory of Executive Function (BRIEF) in Adolescents with Attention Deficit/Hyperactivity Disorder (ADHD). *Child Neuropsychology*, *15*(1), 53-72.

Vloet, T. D., Konrad, K., Herpetz-Dahlmann, B., Polier, G. G. and Günter, T. (2010). Impact of anxiety disorders on attentional functions in children with ADHD. *Journal of Affective Disorders*, *124* (3), 283–290.

Wechsler, D. (2005). *The Wechsler Intelligence Scale for Children- 4th edition.* London: Pearson Assessment.

Willcutt, E. G., Sonuga-Barke, E. J. S., Nigg, J. T. and Sergeant, J. A. (2008). Recent developments in neuropsychological models of childhood disorders. *Advances in Biological Psychiatry*, *24*, 195-226.

Willcutt, E. G. (2012). The prevalence of DSM-IV Attention-Deficit/ Hyperactivity Disorder: A meta-analytic review. *Neurotherapeutics*, *9*(3), 490-499.

Wilson, M. (2008). From processing efficiency to attentional control: a mechanistic account of the anxiety-performance relationship. *International Review of Sport and Exercise Psychology*, *1*(2), 184-201.

Biographical Sketch

Name: Marisol Fernández Cueli

Affiliation: Department of Psychology, University of Oviedo

Date of Birth: 10-August-1986

Education: PhD in Psychology

Address: Department of Psychology, University of Oviedo. Plaza Feijoo s/n, 33003, Oviedo, Spain.

Research and Professional Experience: Associate professor at the University of Oviedo

Publications Last 3 Years:

Marisol Cueli, Paloma González-Castro, Luis Álvarez, Trinidad García and Julio Antonio González-Pienda. (2014). Variables afectivo-motivacionales y rendimiento en matemáticas: un análisis bidireccional. *Revista Mexicana de Psicología, 31*(2), 153-163.

Marisol Cueli, Paloma González-Castro, Jennifer Krawec, José Carlos Núñez y Julio Antonio González-Pienda. (2016). Hipatia: a hypermedia learning environment in mathematic *Anales de Psicología, 32*(1), 98-105.

Marisol Cueli, Paloma González-Castro, Celestino Rodríguez, José Carlos Núñez y Julio Antonio González-Pienda. (In press). Título: Intervención sobre las variables afectivo-motivacionales relacionadas con el aprendizaje en matemáticas. *Educación XX1.*

Marisol Cueli, Celestino Rodríguez, Trinidad García, Débora Areces & Paloma González-Castro. (2015). Título: Experimental study on neurobiofeedback: improved ADHD concentration through nirHEG and blood fluidity. *Revista de Psicología clínica con niños y adolescentes, 2*(2), 9-21.

Name: Paloma González Castro

Affiliation: Department of Psychology, University of Oviedo

Date of Birth: 07-January-1968

Education: PhD in Psychology

Address: Department of Psychology, University of Oviedo. Plaza Feijoo s/n, 33003, Oviedo, Spain.

Research and Professional Experience: Lecturer at the University of Oviedo

Professional Appointments:

Honors:

Publications Last 3 Years:

Paloma González-Castro, Celestino Rodríguez, Ángel López, Marisol Cueli and Luis Álvarez. (2013). Attention Deficit Hyperactivity Disorder, differential diagnosis with blood oxygenation, beta/theta ratio, and attention measures. *International Journal of Clinical and Health Psychology, 13*(2), 101-109

Paloma González-Castro, Celestino Rodríguez, Marisol Cueli, Lourdes Cabeza and Luis Álvarez. (2014). Math Competence and Executive Control Skills in Students with Attention Deficit/Hyperactivity Disorder and Mathematics Learning Disabilities. Revista de *Psicodidáctia, 19*(1), 125-143.

Paloma González-Castro, Marisol Cueli, Lourdes Cabeza, David Álvarez-García & Luis Álvarez. (2014). Improving basic math skills through integrated dynamic representation strategies. Psicothema, 26(3), 378-384

Paloma González-Castro, Celestino Rodríguez, Marisol Cueli, Trinidad García and David Álvarez-García. (2015). State, trait anxiety and selective attention differences in Attention Deficit Hyperactivity Disorder (ADHD) subtypes. *International Journal of Clinical and Health Psychology, 15*(2), 105-112.

Paloma González-Castro, Marisol Cueli, Celestino Rodríguez, Trinidad García and Luis Álvarez. (In press). Efficacy of neurofeedback versus pharmacological support in subjects with ADHD. *Applied Psychophysiology and Biofeedback.*

Name: Trinidad García

Affiliation: Department of Psychology, University of Oviedo

Date of Birth: 12-March-1986

Education: PhD in Psychology

Address: Department of Psychology, University of Oviedo. Plaza Feijoo s/n, 33003, Oviedo, Spain.

Research and Professional Experience: Associate professor at the University of Oviedo

Professional Appointments:

Honors:

Publications Last 3 Years:

García, T., Rodríguez, C., González-Castro, P., González-Pienda, J. A. and Torrance, M. (In Press). Elementary students' metacognitive processes and post-performance calibration on mathematical problem-solving tasks. *Metacognition and Learning, 10,* 2.

García, T., Rodríguez, C., González-Castro, P., Álvarez-García, D. and González-Pienda, J. A. (In Press). Metacognition and executive functions in Primary School. *Annals of Psychoology.*

García, T., González-Castro, P., Rodriguez, C., Cueli, M., Álvarez-García, D. and Álvarez, L. (2014). Executive Functions impairments in ADHD and its subtypes. *Psicología Educativa, 20,* 23 - 32.

García, T., Álvarez-Garcia, D., González-Castro, P., Álvarez, L. and Segurola, L. A. (2014). Psychometric Properties of the Executive Functioning Scale for Teachers (EFS-T). *Revista de Psicología y Educación, 9*(1), 49 – 69.

García, T., Rodríguez, C., González-Castro, P., Álvarez, D., Cueli, M. and González-Pienda, J. A. (2013). Executive Functions in children and adolescent with Attention Deficit Hyperactivity Disorder and Reading Difficulties. *International Journal of Psychology and Psychological Therapy, 13*(2), 179 194.

Name: Débora Areces
Affiliation: Department of Psychology, University of Oviedo
Date of Birth: 04-August-1990
Education: PhD student in Psychology
Address: Department of Psychology, University of Oviedo. Plaza Feijoo s/n, 33003, Oviedo, Spain.

Research and Professional Experience: PhD student at the University of Oviedo

Publications Last 3 Years:

Cueli, M., Rodríguez, C., García, T., Areces, D. and González-Castro, P. (2015). An experimental study on Neurobiofeedback: concentration improvement in ADHD through nirHEG and blood flow activation. *Revista de Psicología Clínica con Niños y Adolescentes. 2*(2), 9-21.

García, T., González-Castro, P., Areces, D., Cueli, M. and Rodríguez, C. (2014). Executive functions in children and adolescents: the types of assessment measures used and implications for their validity in clinical and educational contexts. *Papeles del Psicólogo, 35*(3), 215-223.

García, T., Rodríguez, C., González-Castro, P. and Areces, D. (2014). Executive Functions and their assessment in Children and Adolescents. *Cognitive Sciences, 9*(2), 102-116.

Rodríguez, C., Areces, D., García, T., Cueli, M., Loew, S.J. and González-Castro, P. (2015). ADHD and writing learning disabilities, overlapping and educational implications. *Insights on Learning Disabilities, 12*(2), 121-146

Name: Dr Stephen John Loew
Affiliation: University of New England, Armidale, Australia
Date of Birth: 18/4/57
Education: PhD, BSc(Hons)
Address: 16 Clemenceau Crescent, Tanilba Bay, NSW 2319, Australia

Research and Professional Experience:

2014: Visiting Researcher - International joint-research study *(Fluorescent lighting, ultra-white paper: effects on reading discomfort in 1st-year nursing students) Sunway University, Malaysia.*

2010 – 2014: PhD Research Project

School of Science & Technology, *University of New England, Armidale, Australia*

2014: Visiting Researcher - International Collaborative Research Project *(Levels of visual stress in expert readers; Effects of spectral-filtering), Sunway University, Selangor, Malaysia.*

2013: Visiting Researcher - International Collaborative Research Project *(Levels of visual stress in expert readers; Effects of spectral-filtering), Sunway University, Selangor, Malaysia.*

2013: Short-Term Research Attachment (3 months)

Faculty of Psychology, *University of Oviedo, Asturias, Spain.*

2008 – 2009: BSc Honours Research Project

School of Science & Technology, *University of New England, Armidale, Australia*

Professional Appointments:

2006 – 2007: Chief-Investigator/Research Asst. to Head of School of Science & Technology,

Centre for Bioactive Discovery in Health & Ageing, *University of New England, Australia*

Honors:

Golden Key International Honour Society - (Life-time membership "In Recognition of: Outstanding Scholastic Achievement and Excellence," September, 2005).

Publications Last 3 Years:

Loew, S.J., Rodríguez, C., Marsh, N.V., Jones, G.L., Núñez, J.C. and Watson, K. (2015). Levels of visual stress in proficient readers: effects of spectral filtering of fluorescent lighting on reading discomfort. *Spanish Journal of Psychology, 18,* 1-11.

Loew, S.J., Jones, G.L. and Watson, K. (2014). Meares-Irlen/visual stress syndrome, classroom fluorescent lighting and reading difficulties: a review of the literature. *Insights on Learning Disabilities, 11,* 129-169.

Loew S.J., Marsh, N.V. and Watson, K. (2014). The prevalence of symptoms of visual stress/Meares-Irlen syndrome in subjects diagnosed with chronic fatigue syndrome. *International Journal of Clinical and Health Psychology, 14,* 87-92.

Loew, S.J., Fernández E. and Watson, K. (2013). Incidence of Meares-Irlen/visual stress syndrome in reading and learning disorders: does fluorescent lighting in classrooms affect literacy and numeracy? *Aula Abierte, 41,* 23-32.

Loew, S.J. and Watson, K. (2013). The prevalence of scotopic sensitivity/Meares-Irlen syndrome in subjects diagnosed with ADHD: does misdiagnosis play a role? *Croatian Review of Rehabilitation Research, 49,* 50-58.

Loew, S.J. and Watson, K. (2012). *Spectral filtering of fluorescent lighting: effects upon reading and visual discomfort in slow readers.* In: J.A. Gonzalez-Pienda, C. Rodriguez, D. Alvarez, R. Cerezo, E. Fernandez, M. Cueli, T. Garcia, E. Tuero and Suarez, N. (Eds.), Learning Disabilities: Present and Future. Oviedo: Learning Disabilities WorldWide, Pp. 267-278.

Loew, S.J. and Watson, K. (2012). A prospective genetic marker of the visual-perception disorder Meares-Irlen syndrome. *Perceptual and Motor Skills, 114,* 870-882.

Rodríguez, C., Areces, D., García, T., Cueli, M., **Loew, S.J. and** González-Castro, P. (2015). ADHD and writing learning disabilities: overlapping disorders and educational implications. *Insights on Learning Disabilities, 12, 121-146.*

Iglesias-García, M.T., Gutiérrez-Fernández, N., **Loew, S.** and Rodríguez, C. (2016 in press). Hábitos y técnicas de estudio en adolescentes con Trastorno por Déficit de Atención con o sin Hiperactividad (TDAH). *European Journal of Education and Psychology.*

Short-Bio: I am a biological scientist whose primary research interests are the epidemiology of Meares-Irlen/visual stress syndrome, the overlap of symptoms with ADHD and other disorders, and the effects of fluorescent lighting upon literacy and learning in general. My research in these areas has been published in a number of peer-reviewed journals and has also been presented at several international conferences. I have recently completed a wide-ranging PhD research project investigating biophysical and genetic factors in *visual stress*, its role in declining rates of student literacy and numeracy, and whether increasingly brighter fluorescent lighting has enhanced that role. I am also one of the few (if any) researchers of *visual stress* who actually has the condition himself, and this has undoubtedly contributed to my reputation for novel research ideas and insights relating to reading and attention disorders.

Name: Celestino Rodríguez Pérez
Affiliation: Department of Psychology, University of Oviedo
Date of Birth: 25-January-1980
Education: PhD in Psychology
Address: Department of Psychology, University of Oviedo. Plaza Feijoo s/n, 33003, Oviedo, Spain.

Research and Professional Experience: Assistant at the University of Oviedo

Publications Last 3 Years:

Trinidad García, Celestino Rodríguez, Paloma González-Castro, David Álvarez, Marisol Cueli and Julio Antonio González-Pienda. (2013). Funciones ejecutivas en niños y adolescentes con trastornos por déficit de atención con hiperactividad y dificultades lectoras. *International Journal of Psychology & Psychological Therapy, 13*(2), 179-194

Paloma González-Castro, Celestino Rodríguez, Ángel López, Marisol Cueli and Luis Álvarez. (2013). Attention Deficit Hyperactivity Disorder, differential diagnosis with blood oxygenation, beta/theta ratio, and attention measures. *International Journal of Clinical and Health Psychology, 13*(2), 101-109

Paloma González-Castro, Celestino Rodríguez, Marisol Cueli, Lourdes Cabeza and Luis Álvarez. (2014). Math Competence and Executive Control Skills in Students with Attention Deficit/Hyperactivity Disorder and Mathematics Learning Disabilities. Revista de *Psicodidáctia, 19*(1), 125-143.

Trinidad García, Celestino Rodríguez, Paloma González-Castro, Luis Álvarez and Marisol Cueli. (2014). La atención y el sacádico: Efectos clínicos en el Trastorno por Déficit de Atención con Hiperactividad (TDAH). Revista Iberoamericana de Psicología y Salud, 5(1), 1-21

Paloma González-Castro, Celestino Rodríguez, Marisol Cueli, Trinidad García and David Álvarez-García. (2015). State, trait anxiety and selective attention differences in Attention Deficit Hyperactivity Disorder (ADHD)

subtypes. *International Journal of Clinical and Health Psychology, 15*(2), 105-112.

Marisol Cueli, Celestino Rodríguez, Trinidad García, Débora Areces & Paloma González-Castro. (2015). Título: Experimental study on neurobiofeedback: improved ADHD concentration through nirHEG and blood fluidity. *Revista de Psicología clínica con niños y adolescentes, 2*(2), 9-21.

In: Trait and State Anxiety
Editor: Abel Bradley
ISBN: 978-1-63484-840-4

Chapter 4

THE COMBINATION OF HIGH TRAIT ANXIETY AND FEMALE SEX IS VULNERABILITY FACTOR FOR SLEEP DISTURBANCES

Yulia Arapova* and Evgeniy Verbitsky
Department of Physiology,
Institute of Arid Zones of the Southern Scientific Center,
Institution of the Russian Academy of Science, Russia

ABSTRACT

One hundred and ten healthy volunteers, men and women undergraduates from 19 to 25 years of age took part in preliminary survey. According to survey data sixty four participants with low and high trait anxiety completed one night of home-based polysomnography, the sleep structure was drawn and electroencephalography analysis was done. The shorter sleep duration, more time awake, less delta-sleep and less REM stage without signs of subsequent compensation were found among individuals of high trait anxiety. In addition to that the lower theta power in high anxious men and lower delta power, higher alpha and beta

* Corresponding author: Yulia Arapova, Department of Physiology, Institute of Arid Zones of the Southern Scientific Center, Institution of the Russian Academy of Science 41 Chekhov str., Rostov-on-Don, 344006, Russia, Tel/Fax: 007 863 2509813/007 863 2665677, E-mail: juli.arapova@yandex.ru.

powers in anxious women in delta-sleep were obtained. The lower theta power in REM stage for anxious individuals was displayed. As a result, an anxious women are more vulnerable to the sleep disturbances than anxious men.

Keywords: trait anxiety, men, women, sleep, EEG

Introduction

In this study we used concept of anxiety suggested by Spielberger (1985), according to which trait anxiety is a personality trait associated to expectations of overt-affect/ambiguous-affect stimuli even in the neutral condition (Bradley et al., 1998; Bishop et al., 2004; Barlow, 2002; Matthews et al., 2011), novel environment, and daily routines on a daily basis as a potentially dangerous (Bishop, 2007), unlike state anxiety when these manifestations are temporary.

In accordance with neurocognitive model (Sandi and Richter-Levin, 2009), high trait anxiety individuals tend to perceive moderate events as stressful and their neuropsychological responses to negative stimuli are stronger and more long-lasting than responses in low anxious individuals (Willmann et al., 2012). It has been surmised that high anxious individuals display difficulty in emotional expression recognition and they have alteration at the early stages of information processing, which lead to deficit of involuntary emotional detection at its later stages (Walentowska and Wronka, 2012). It concerns the reduction of the prefrontal-amygdala functional connectivity (Kim and Whalen, 2009) and neurocognitive dysfunctions in structures of a brain involved into generation of arousal and emotional responses (Eysenck, 1992; Clark, 1999; Shin et al., 2001; Koo et al., 2004; Beck et al., 1985).

The other features of attentional system of high anxious individuals are preparedness for processing of information in unfamiliar environment (Knyazev et al., 2006) and retention of strong and long-lasting responses to negative and stressful stimuli, so the reaction of habituation to the repeated auditory stimuli is not registered or it comes later in high anxious subjects (Savost'ianov and Savost'ianova, 2003; Martin-Soelch et al., 2006). Interestingly, that this effect is widely expressed among high anxious women, who experience difficulty in disengaging attention from the location threat-related stimuli in the unconscious condition, while high anxious man show attentional avoidance of it (Tan et al., 2011; Putman, 2011). According to the "two hit hypothesis" (Beck et al., 2010; Sheynina et al., 2014; Catuzzi and Beck, 2014) anxious females possess not only attentional bias to threat stimuli similar to anxious men, but they also show behavioral inhibition characterized by response inflexibility to stimuli. Moreover, high anxious females show higher level of worry and emotionality (Everson and Millsar, 1991). So females are more anxious than men (McLean and Anderson, 2009).

In any way, trait anxiety may be as a predictor of anxiety disorders, depressions progress, and disorders that spread more likely among women (Breslau et al., 1997; Bangasser, 2013; Craske, 2003). A neurocognitive functions disorder anxiety and depression are often accompanied by sleep disorders (Vahtera et al., 2007; Killgore, 2013). The impairment of night sleep of high trait anxiety persons isn't so dramatically as in people who suffer from depression or anxiety disorders (Breslau et al., 1996; Hita-Yañez et al., 2013), but it may have the same pattern (Rosa et al., 1983; Breslau et al., 1996; Gau, 2000).

Despite obvious combination of trait high anxiety and the risk of having insomnia and anxiety disorders (Hettema, 2008; Sandi and Richter-Levin, 2009), the pattern of dream in people with high level of trait anxiety, who are actually in good health, are poorly studied.

The aim of the present study was to verify the possible existence of gender differences in sleep organization of individuals with low and high trait anxiety levels.

METHODS

Participants

One hundred ten healthy volunteers, men and women, who are undergraduates from 19 to 25 years old, took part in preliminary survey to avoid their sleep disorders, hospital anxiety and depression. The study in accordance with ethical standards of the Declaration of Helsinki (1964) has been performed. Every person prior to their inclusion in the study gave their written consent. To avoid the risk of sleep disorders or clinical anxiety they filled in the following questionnaires: Sleep Quality Survey (Veyn and Hecht, 1989), Sleep Apnea Scale (Elegulashvily, 1997), Epworth Sleepiness Scale (Johns, 1991), Hospital Anxiety and Depression Scale (Zigmond and Snaith, 1983). The Sleep Quality Survey (Veyn and Hecht, 1989) contains items about falling asleep, sleep time, night awakening, dreams, morning awakening. Sleep

Apnea Scale (Elegulashvily, 1997) includes questions about appearances of snoring, intermittent snoring, sleepiness during activity, morning hypertension, morning thirst and morning headache.

Russian versions of the Spielberger State Trait Anxiety Inventory (STAI, Spielberger, 1985), Cattel 16 Personality Factors for adults (Cattell et al., 1970), the Taylor Manifest Anxiety Scale (MAS, Taylor, 1953) were used as psychometric measures of anxiety. The data of the investigation were analyzed using Factor analysis that gave opportunity to determine which scales of surveys are determinant for the factor appropriate for level of trait anxiety (basing on scales of STAI). Scales of surveys grouped factors were used in Cluster analysis grounding on which results the participants were divided into three groups considering different levels of trait anxiety. This complex assessment of level of personal anxiety was chosen to improve representativeness of sampling of individuals with high and low trait anxiety. For further analysis we built quite similar groups in number of examined: the group of low trait anxiety consisting of 12 men and 12 women and the group of high trait anxiety consisting of 20 men and 20 women.

Procedures

Subjects with low and high levels of trait anxiety participated in polysomnography study. There were 12 men and 12 women with low level of trait anxiety, and 20 men and 20 women with the high one. The participants had comfortable sleep at their houses for one night at their habitual sleep and wake times; all participants went to bed at 9 p.m., and they might watched TV, read book, etc. prior to fall asleep.

Night sleep was recorded with a LEONARDO polygraph (Medizintechnik, Germany). Electroencephalogram bilateral central (C3 and C4), parietal (P3 and P4), and occipital (O1 and O2) sites, refererred to A1+A2, bilateral electrooculogram (left and right), electromyogram of the sublingual muscle, electrocardiogram, and respiratory rate, with simultaneous videomonitoring according to AASM rules were recorded (Iber et al., 2007). Unipolar registration of EEG signals in pass band of 0.5 and 30 Hz with sample rate of 500 Hz. A 50 Hz notch filter attenuated electrical noise.

2.4. Data processing and Statistical analyses

Sleep was visually staged by three experts according to standard criteria (Rechtschaffen and Kales, 1968; Iber et al., 2007). Artifacts were eliminated from analysis. The total time of sleep (periods of wake were excluded), sleep latency (as a time from light-out and initial presence of stage 2), REM latency (as a time from sleep onset to initial presence of first REM period), time awake after sleep onset (as the total minutes from sleep onset to wake-up) were measured. Percentages of stage 2, delta-sleep and REM stage were determined by dividing the total amount of time in each of these stages by the total sleep time. These parameters were calculated for all period of night sleep and particularly for first free cycles of the sleep.

EEG spectral power was calculated using fast Fourier transform (FFT analysis) in four conventional frequency categories: delta (0.5 to < 4.0 Hz), theta (4.0 to < 8.0 Hz), alpha (8.0 to < 12.0 Hz), beta (12.0 to < 20.0 Hz). FFT was calculated in delta-sleep and REM stage for first cycle of the sleep. Consequent analyses with log-transformed spectral power were performed.

The data were analyzed using the Statistica 8 software. The following statistic methods of data processing were carried out: Factor Analysis, Cluster Analysis, Analysis of covariance (ANCOVA), t-test for independent samples, Kraskal-Wallis test. Analyses process further in the results is described.

RESULTS

Participants

Factor and Cluster Analyses were performed for the division of the 110 subjects with different levels of trait anxiety by the groups. Factor analysis for determining of the least number of characteristics that belong to a certain level of trait anxiety was carried out. For the psychological assessment of each participant the following items were selected from raw scores of each individual: sixteen primary factors and four secondary factors of the Cattel 16 Personality Factors for adults (factors and codes name are following: A,B,C,E,F,G,H,I,L,M,N,O,Q1,Q2,Q3,Q4,F1,F2,F3,F4), scales of trait (code name TA), and state anxiety (code name SA) of the STAI and scale of the MAS (code name MAS). Initially, the factorability of the 23 items was examined. It was determined that O, O4, F1, TA, SA, and MAS variables are highly correlated with each other, but not to the rest of the variables. F, H, F2 variables are highly correlated with each other, but not to the rest of the variables. And A, F3 variables are highly correlated with each other, but not to the rest of the variables. Thus, with the help of eleven variables one can measure three factors of our interest. The sampling adequacy was calculated by Bartletts Test of Sphericity (Chi-sqr. = 239.04, df = 187, $p > .05$). The number of factor to retain was based on the Cattell's scree plot. Method Varimax raw was used for the factor rotation.

Three factors were allocated. The Factor 1 has eigenvalue of 5.920 (25.74% variant explained), Factor 2 obtains 3.88 (16.86% variant explained), and Factor 3 has 2.70 (11.75% variant explained).

Table 1. Rotated component matrix

Variable	Factor 1	Factor 2	Factor 3
A	0.142	0.154	**0.775**
B	0.389	0.290	-0.097
C	-0.401	0.414	-0.172
E	-0.221	0.332	-0.323
F	-0.129	**0.713**	0.049
G	0.070	0.173	0.492
H	-0.208	**0.815**	0.138
I	-0.169	0.156	0.276
L	0.243	0.308	-0.498
M	-0.081	0.201	0.435
N	0.012	-0.427	0.224
O	**0.897**	-0.017	-0.022
Q1	-0.257	0.391	0.490
Q2	-0.277	-0.427	0.051
Q3	0.155	0.142	0.336
Q4	**0.860**	-0.044	0.150
F1	**0.862**	-0.282	-0.058
F2	-0.132	**0.887**	0.151
F3	-0.059	-0.020	**-0.766**
F4	-0.177	-0.402	-0.411
TA	**0.911**	0.012	-0.038
ST	**0.887**	-0.083	0.070
Teylor	**0.920**	0.053	-0.046

Note: Extraction Method is Principial Component Analysis. Text highlight indicates factor loading >.07.

Table 2. Analysis of variance

Variable	Distance between groups	df	Distance within group	df	F	Signif. p
O	135.95	2	36.60	26	48.27	0.000000
Q4	51.98	2	44.57	26	15.15	0.000043
F1	53.30	2	35.26	26	19.64	0.000006
TA	4161.88	2	921.98	26	58.68	0.000000
SA	1554.56	2	671.64	26	30.08	0.000000
MAS	2605.07	2	168.37	26	201.13	0.000000

Note: O, O4, Fl = factors of the Cattel 16 Personality Factors for adults. TA = scale of trait anxiety and SA = scale of state anxiety of the STAI. MAS = scale of the MAS

Table 3. Means (SE) of scales of the survey

	Cattel 16 Personality Factors			STAI		Taylor MAS
	O	Q4	F1	TA	ST	MAS
Men with high trait anxiety, N = 20	9.17 (0.38)	7.17 (0.29)	7.13 (0.38)	52.83 (1.89)	55.17 (1.26)	28.5 (0.82)
Women with high trait anxiety, N = 20	8.00 (0.29)	6.31 (0.16)	6.54 (0.20)	52.14 (1.49)	48.71 (0.87)	26.14 (0.40)
Men with low trait anxiety, N = 12	3.34 (0.14)	2.32 (0.37)	4.23 (0.14)	20.34 (1.16)	37.34 (1.50)	4.20 (0.24)
Women with low trait anxiety, N = 12	3.40 (0.26)	4.10 (0.42)	3.30 (0.37)	26.81 (0.54)	34.40 (1.29)	4.20 (0.97)

Table 1 shows six items that loaded onto Factor 1, they described various manifestations of anxiety, i.e., factor O = Apprehension, factor Q4 = Tension, factor F1 = Anxiety, and factor TA = determined level of trait anxiety, factor ST = determined level of state anxiety, factor MAS = determined anxiety. Three items loaded onto Factor 2 related to liveliness (factor F), social boldness (factor H) and extraversion (factor F2). The two items that belonged to Factor 3 identified warmth (factor A) and balance of emotionality (factor F3).

Grouping of examined people according to the level of the trait anxiety were done on the basis of results of Cluster analysis in tag field determined by the first factor of the Factor Analysis. Analysis with the help of K-means

Clustering method was carried out. As our main task was to split the examined people to three groups of low, average and high level of anxiety. Calculation of distance between clusters on constant intervals was carried out. Euclidian distance between the first and the second clusters was 9.88, between the first cluster and the third one was 7.01, between the second and the third one was 16.4. Table 2 shows means of intergroup and intragroup dispersions of features, and it appears that TA, SA, MAS was the most featured to the clusters under investigation. Grounding the analysis all examined belonged to 3 clusters; analyzing clusters' data and basing on value of the tests' results (Cattell et al., 1970; Spielberger, 1985; Taylor, 1953) it was ascertained that first cluster included the persons with moderate trait anxiety, second one included people with high trait anxiety, and the third cluster includes those with low trait anxiety. We builted quite similar groups in number of examined; those groups was the group of low trait anxiety consisting of 12 men and 12 women and the group of high trait anxiety consisting of 20 men and 20 women. Average values of factors on the basis of which the examined were grouped into clusters are given in the table 3.

All Night Sleep Architecture

The effects of Sex and Anxiety using analysis of covariance (ANCOVA) were calculated. The Sex was used as a fixed factor (the legend: 1 = men, 2 = women), and Anxiety as a continuous covariate (the legend: 1 = low trait anxiety, 2 = high trait anxiety). Dependent variables was sleep duration, sleep latency, REM latency, time awake after sleep onset, amount of movements and duration of the 2 stage, delta-sleep, and REM sleep. According to statistical data the significant influences of factor Sex ($F(8, 56) = 6.7$; $p < .001$) on sleep parameters were shown and the variation of sleep parameters depended on level of trait anxiety ($F(8, 56) = 62.4$; $p < .001$).

Table 4 presents sleep measures for men and women low and high in trait anxiety. It was established statistically significant differences for quantitative sleep measures between individuals (Bonferroni correction for T-test), which revealed that high anxious men had shorter sleep duration ($t = 4.2$, $p > .001$), more time awake during sleep ($t = 4.7$, $p > .0002$), shorter delta-sleep ($t = 3.9$, $p = .001$), and shorter REM stage ($t = 4.4$, $p > .001$) in comparison to low trait anxious men. The high trait anxious women had shorter sleep duration ($t = 4.4$, $p > 0.001$), more time awake ($t = 6.1$, $p < .001$), less delta-sleep ($t = 8.5$, $p < .001$), and REM stage ($t = 6.8$, $p > .001$) than those of low trait anxious.

Besides, low anxious men had less amount of movements ($t = 2.8$, $p > .001$), but more time awake during sleep ($t = 4.1$, $p > .001$) than low anxious women had. The high anxious men have less time awake ($t = 2.9$, $p = 0.01$), less amount of movements ($t = 3.4$, $p = .002$) and more delta-sleep ($t = 3.2$, $p > .001$) than high anxious women had.

Table 4. Sleep measures in men and women with different levels of trait anxiety

	Men		Women	
	LA	HA	LA	HA
TST, min, mean (SD)	501.7(41.2)	421.9(36.7)[a]	526.1(52.6)	381.8(68.3)[b]
Sleep latency, min, mean (SD)	6.9(2.6)	13.0(6.6)	8.5(3.1)	26.3(17.7)
Awake after sleep onset, min, mean (SD)	15.0(2.4)[d]	26.8(6.3)[a, c]	7.1(3.8)	40.7(12.9)[b]
Amount of movements, mean (SD)	13.5(6.3)[d]	15.2(7.0)[c]	28.3(13.2)	26.2(12.1)
REM latency, min, mean (SD)	118.1(24.2)	82.4(22.7)	121.0(34.2)	134.6(65.5)
2 stage NREM, min, mean (SD), % of TST	204.4(60.9) 40.7	224.5(40.9) 53.2	237.9(52.5) 45.2	229.8(62.4) 60.1
Delta-sleep, min, mean (SD), % of TST	127.9(22.3) 25.5	79.3(27.4)[a,c] 18.7	112.6(12.6) 21.4	58.1(10.3)[b] 15.2
REM stage, min, mean (SD), % of TST	139.7(33.0) 27.8	84.9(16.6)[a,] 20.1	142.5(21.4) 27.1	66.8(21.4)[b] 17.5

Note: LA = individuals with low trait anxiety level. HA = individuals with high trait anxiety level. TST = Total sleep time. REM = Rapid eye movement sleep. NREM = Nonrapid eye movement sleep.

[a] Significant differences HA men with LA men, respectively.

[b] Significant differences HA women with LA women, respectively.

[c] Significant differences HA men with HA women.

[d] Significant differences LA men with LA women.

Awake, Delta-Sleep, and REM Stage Representation in the Three Parts of an Individual's Sleep

Analysis of change of sleepless periods, delta-sleep and REM stage of the first three cycles of sleep of examined men and women, which had high and low levels of anxiety with Kruskal-Wallis test (multiple comparisons with Bonferroni correction, in which $p < .017$) was implemented. Further we described only significant alterations; the data of analyses at the table 5 are presented. The shortening of delta-sleep duration from the first to the third cycle of sleep and increase of REM stage in the second cycle of sleep of men with low level of trait anxiety was found out. High trait anxious men showed increase of REM stage from the first to the third cycle. Women who had low level of trait anxiety in the third cycle of sleep had shorter delta-sleep, but REM stage was longer than in the first cycle of sleep. Women with high level of trait anxiety in the third cycle had longer REM stage, and time awake was lower than of the first cycle.

Table 5. Sleepless periods, delta-sleep and REM stage of the first three cycles of sleep in men and women with different levels of trait anxiety

	Men		**Women**	
	LA	**HA**	**LA**	**HA**
Delta-sleep duration, min				
1st cycle of sleep	74.7(13.4)	39.6(24.1)	71.6(8.9)	31.7(26.3)
2nd cycle of sleep	31.2(14.2)	26.4(14.3)	24.7(7.9)	27.1(17.9)
3rd cycle of sleep	16.7(7.1)	36.6(16.7)	19.5(4.8)	12.2(5.1)
Kruskal-Wallis test	H(2, = 36) = 18.0; p <. 001)	H(2, = 60) = 3.2; p = .2)	H(2, = 36) = 9.9; p < .01)	H(2, = 60) = 4.6; p = .09)
REM stage duration, min				
1st cycle of sleep	17.8(9.2)	13.8(4.6)	17.7(9.6)	12.8(9.3)
2nd cycle of sleep	57.1(22.)	29.3(12.5)	39.4(12.5)	23.9(12.0)
3rd cycle of sleep	58.7(22.3)	38.9(16.7)	69.9(16.5)	50.7(25.3)
Kruskal-Wallis test	H(2, =36) = 14.5; p < .001)	H(2, = 60) = 13.8; p =.001)	H(2, = 36) = 7.2; p=.01)	H(2, = 60) = 15.4; p < .001)
Sleepless periods duration, min				
1st cycle of sleep	7.3(4.4)	13.3(7.2)	5.1(2.9)	23.1(14.1)
2nd cycle of sleep	4.0(3.1)	9.9(6.4)	1.5(0.5)	12.3(9.7)
3rd cycle of sleep	7.9(4.8)	7.1(4.2)	3.0(1.3)	3.3(1.5)
Kruskal-Wallis test	H(2, = 36) = 2.2; p = .3)	H(2, = 60) = 7.3; p = .02)	H(2, = 36) = 3.1; p = .2)	H(2, = 60) = 12.1; p =.002)

Note: LA = individuals with low trait anxiety level. HA = individuals with high trait anxiety level.

Personal Anxiety Characteristics of the Sleep EEG

To discard inter hemispheric differences the average power measures over homological left and right areas were used in subsequent analysis. Analysis of covariance (ANCOVA) was used to test the effects of Sex and Anxiety on the EEG spectral power. The Sex was used as a fixed factor (the legend: 1 = men, 2 = women), and Anxiety as a continuous covariate (the legend: 1=low trait anxiety, 2 = high trait anxiety). Dependent variables were average delta, theta, alpha, and beta power over homological left and right central, occipital and parietal areas. Results of the analysis discovered statistically significant influence of factor Sex ($F(12, 147) = 9.7$; $p < .0001$) on variations of considered power (EEG spectral power), yet the power possesses statistical significance for the level of personal trait anxiety ($F(12, 147) = 5.2$; $p < .0001$).

To revealed significant difference of spectral power of delta, theta, alpha, and beta power in delta-sleep and REM stage between men with high and low levels of trait anxiety, women with high and low levels of trait anxiety, between men and women with low level of trait anxiety, and men and women with high level of trait anxiety Bonferroni correction for T-test was applied.

Figure 1 displays that during delta-sleep low anxious men had theta power higher at central, $t = 2.9$; $p = .001$ and at parietal, $t = 5.7$; $p = .0001$, and at occipital, $t = 4.2$; $p = .001$ areas. The delta power spectrum of low anxious women was found higher at central areal, $t = 2.8$; $p = .001$, alpha power was lower at parietal, $t = 5.6$; $p = .001$ and occipital, $t = 3.3$; $p=.001$ sites, and beta power lower at parietal area, $t = 2.7$; $p = .007$, and differed from those that high anxious women had.

Low anxious men had lower delta power at central ($t = 2.8$; $p = .001$), parietal ($t = 3.3$; $p = .006$), and occipital ($t = 4.1$; $p = .0002$) areas than low anxious women had. High anxious men showed the lower delta power at parietal, $t = 4.5$; $p = .0001$ and occipital, $t = 2.7$; $p = .001$ areas, lower theta power at parietal, $t = 6.7$; $p = .0001$ and occipital, $t = 5.4$; $p=.0001$ areas, and lower alpha power at parietal, $t = 6.5$; $p = .0001$ and occipital, $t = 4.5$; $p = .001$ areas, lower beta power at parietal area, $t = 3.9$; $p = .0002$.

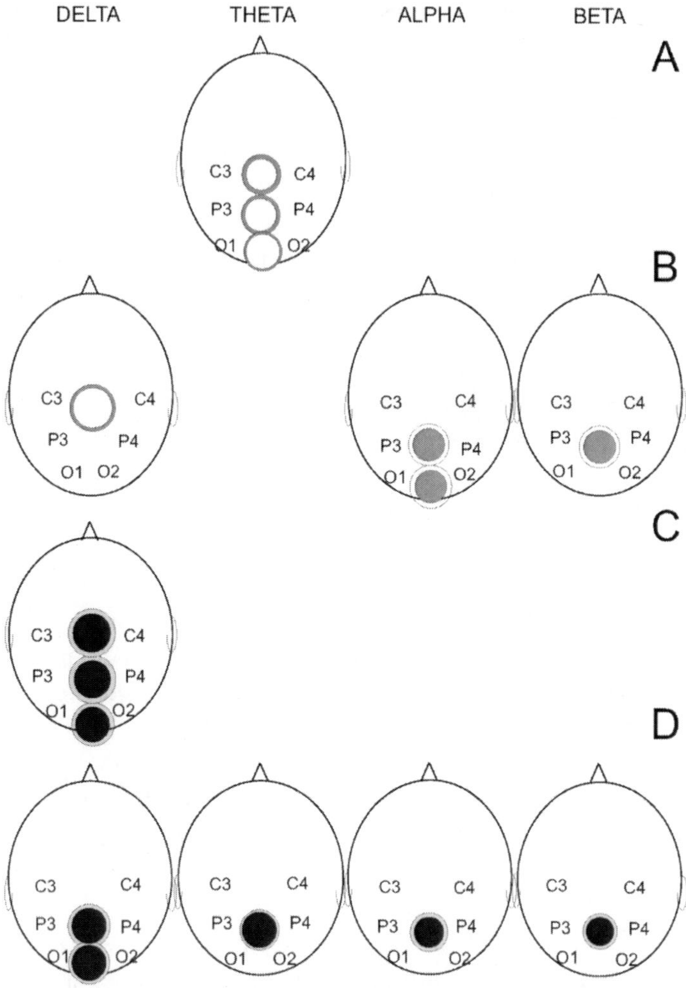

Figure 1. Influence of personal trait anxiety on the EEG power spectrum at central, parietal, occipital areas in delta-sleep. Legend: Picture shows only statistically significant differences. A letter A marks to a significant difference between low anxious and high anxious men. A letter B marks to a significant difference between low anxious and high anxious women. A letter C marks to a significant difference between low anxious men and low anxious women. A letter D marks to a significant difference between high anxious men and high anxious women. Low anxious individuals = grey circle, high anxious individuals = white circle in the parts of figure marked letters A and B. Men = black circle, women = grey circle in the parts of figure marked letters C and D. A diameter of the circle corresponds to the power of rhythm.

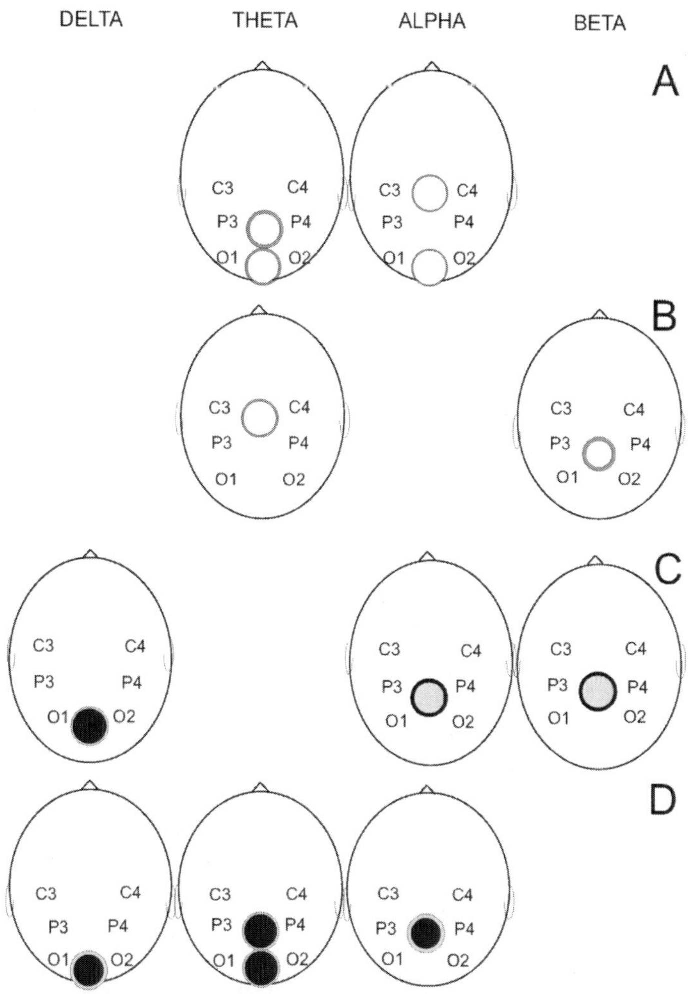

Figure 2. Influence of personal trait anxiety on the EEG power spectrum at central, parietal, occipital areas in REM stage. Legend: the same as to Figure 1.

The figure 2 presents that during REM stage low anxious men had higher theta power at parietal area, $t = 4.1$; $p = .0001$ and occipital one, $t = 4.3$; $p > .0001$, alpha power at central, $t = 3$; $p > .001$, parietal, $t = 5.8$; $p > .0001$, and occipital $t = 4.02$; $p > .0001$ areas. Low anxious women had higher theta power at central area, $t = 3.1$; $p=.002$, and lower beta power at parietal area, $t = 3.4$; $p = .001$. Moreover, low anxious men showed lower delta power at occipital area, $t = 4.7$; $p > .001$, and higher alpha, $t = 4.3$; $p > .0001$ and beta,

$t = 3.2$; $p = .001$ powers at parietal area, than low anxious women did. It was detected that theta, $t = 3.2$; $p > .001$ and alpha, $t = 2.2$; $p > .001$ powers at the parietal area, and delta, $t = 4.9$; $p > .0001$ and theta, $t = 3.5$; $p > .0001$ powers at occipital area were higher in high anxious women than high anxious men had.

DISCUSSION

Thus, we determined that the night sleep of high trait anxious individuals was shorter with often waking ups, had shorter delta-sleep and REM stage comparing to the same parameters of those individuals with low level of anxiety. Similar results about sleep organization of anxious individuals hold for healthy men with different levels of trait anxiety (Rosa et al., 1983; Gau, 2000; Roehrs et al., 1990). On the other hand, current study demonstrated more dramatically sleep structures changes in anxious women that may be predictive for onset sleep disturbances (Vahtera et al., 2007) such as insomnia (Bastien et al., 2008). This similarity may be explained by the fact that both high anxiety and insomnia are related with hyper-arousal round-the-clock (Sysoeva, 2008; Bonnet and Arand, 2010; Feige et al., 2013). Besides, many longitudinal studies suggested that anxious people belong to a risk group of suffering from insomnia (Alvaro et al., 2012). Analysis of a sleep dynamics in its first three cycles showed that men and women of high level of trait anxiety had no changes of delta-sleep length on the background of prolonging of REM stage from the first cycle to the third one. But one found shortening of delta-sleep with further prolonging of REM stage in individuals with low level of trait anxiety. According to the concepts of researchers (Kovrov and Vein, 2004), the first cycle of sleep has priority importance for the development of the entire sleep, since in subsequent cycles of sleep, disturbances of the first cycle are compensated. Despite similar development of sleep stages of all participants, the high anxious individuals (men and women) had lower delta-sleep duration in all cycles of sleep that excluded its subsequent compensation. The mentioned changes in the sleep without signs of subsequent compensation were described in patients with insomniac disorders (Bastien et al., 2008).

We found out that anxious individuals comparing to those with low level of trait anxiety man had lower spectral power in theta powers, women had lower delta and higher one in alpha and beta powers in delta-sleep. In REM stage low trait anxiety men had stronger spectral power in theta, alpha powers than men with high level of anxiety had. Women with low level of anxiety comparing to women with high level of anxiety had stronger spectral power of theta and lower spectral power of beta.

The decrease for absolute cortical activation of NREM and REM sleep of suffering paradoxical insomnia and alterations in sleep macrostructure compared to the good sleepers were revealed (St-Jean et al., 2013). The authors supposed that pre-sleep levels of arousal were linked to sleep quality of the subsequent night (Turcotte and Bastien, 2009). In current study the more variable differences in value power spectrum between high anxious and low anxious individuals than between insomniac and good sleepers were found. It is known, that amount of the slow-wave activity reflects accumulation of sleep need during wakefulness (Borbely, 1982; Dijk et al., 1987; Van Dongen et al., 2003), but it depends also on quality of prior wakefulness, namely of the amount of synaptic plasticity, which occurring during wakefulness (Tononi and Cirelli, 2003; 2006), so the sleep and sleep loss directly influence on cortical plasticity (Frank et al., 2001; Jha et al., 2005). The higher is the level of exploratory behavior during waking up the lager is the slow-wave activity response during sleep (cited by Huber, et al., 2006). According to the data (Henniger et al., 2000; Krömer et al., 2005) the high-anxiety-related animals prefer to use passive strategies of behavior in unfamiliar, negative, and stressor situations. We assume that the lower power in delta-sleep of anxious individuals may reflects their preferences in social behavioral.

Moreover, in this research we revealed gender differences for spectral power in delta-sleep and REM stage. The delta power in delta-sleep was higher in women than in men, and low anxious men in comparison to women had the stronger spectral power of alpha and beta powers and lower delta power in REM stage. The high trait anxious women comparing to men had the strongest spectral power in all ranges under analysis, and in delta-sleep and REM stage. At the present time the role of gender factor in EEG differences within sleep remain uncertain. Dijk et al. (1989) detected higher power densities during NREM and REM sleep over a wide frequency range of women comparing to men. Considering these data, Carrier et al. (2001) found out that women had higher power density than men in delta, theta, low alpha powers, and high spindle frequency range, while Armitage (1995) suggested that men and women had little amplitude EEG distinctions, although the higher delta power in NREM among women was confirmed. In subsequent study Armitage et al. (2000) indicated that EEG did not differ for healthy men and women, but number of depressed patients, the men who had lower delta slow wave power comparing to depressed women and healthy men and women. The lower delta of men comparing to women was found among depressed individuals under investigation (Reynolds et al., 1990). Our results showed that gender differences in power EEG more expressed among high anxious individuals: anxious men had lower power EEG in some frequencies in delta-sleep and REM sleep comparing to women.

CONCLUSION

In the current study we proved that different psychological and physiological features were found to be significantly related with inter-individual differences of trait anxiety. There are strongly reported genetic bases underlying differential neurocognitive mechanisms, which contribute to individual differences in characteristics of the trait anxiety (Bertolino et al., 2005; Heinz et al., 2004). As consistent with hypothesis in differential psychophysiology (Teplov, 1961; Nebylitsin, 1966), the strategy of individual behavioral personal characteristics of nervous system is determined. The published data about neurophysiological mechanisms of anxiety (Davidson, 1990; Chua et al., 1999; Vuilleumeier, 2002; Davis, 1992; Phelps et al., 2001), cognitive, emotional, and behavioral features of anxious person (McNally, 1982; Davidson et al., 1990; Gray, 1994; Aftanas et al., 2004) assumed that anxious individuals had high reactivity and plasticity of the neural processes.

Certainly, most steady traits of the personality and the basic properties of the nervous system may be related with some parameters of EEG (Rusalov, 1979; Veldhuizen et al., 1993; Klimesch, 1999; McEvoy et al., 2001; Finelli et al., 2001; Williams et al., 2005). This individual stability of EEG profiles during wakefulness (McEvoy et al., 2001) and sleep (Williams et al., 2005) are genetically determined (Finelli et al., 2001; Tononi and Cirelli, 2001; Andretic et al., 2008; Buechel et al., 2011). And it was established that neuronal plasticity underlies link between waking activity, particularly exploratory behavior, and the homeostatic sleep responses (Huber et al., 2006). In compliance of novel hypothesis (Tononi and Cirelli, 2003; 2006), a sleep downscales synaptic strength to baseline level, that increases in many brain circuits as a result of flexible processes during wakefulness.

These features of nervous system of anxious individuals may explain their cognitive bias related with processing of information in unfamiliar environment. But the high reactivity and flexibility of the neural processes may lead to the development of cognitive dysfunction and further to the neurological disorders (Nebylitsin, 2000). So in the study we have found sleep alteration of a high trait anxiety person like of a patient with insomnia and depression but we exchanged EEG with NREM and REM sleep typical for these diseases (Buysse et al., 2008) haven't been revealed among trait anxiety individuals. In line with the study (Lindberg et al., 1997), we found out that women suffer more from high trait anxiety then men; higher prevalence of anxious women in the most cases explains the gender differences in sleep complaints (Hirshkowitz et al., 1990; Leger et al., 2009). Thereby, according to the current study the heightened of the trait anxiety related with accumulation of the sleep alterations. Especially it is expressed among females; it means that high anxious women are more vulnerable to the sleep disturbances then men. It may be important in opt for gender therapy anxiety disorders.

REFERENCES

Aftanas, L. I., Pavlov, S. V., Reva, N. V. and Varlamov, A. A. (2004). Event-related synchronization and desynchronization of EEG during appraisal of threatening and pleasant visual stimuli in high anxious subjects. *I.P. Pavlov Journal of Higher Nervous Activity.*, *54*, 473-481.

Alvaro, P. K., Roberts, R. M. and Harris, J. K. (2012). A systematic review assessing biderectionality between sleep disturbances, anxiety, and depression. *Sleep.*, *36*, 1059-1068.

Andretic, R., Franken, P. and Tafti, M. (2008). Genetics of sleep. *Annu. Rev. Genet.*, *42*, 361-388.

Armitage, R. (1995). The Distribution of EEG frequencies in REM and NREM sleep stages in healthy young adults. *Sleep.*, *18*, 334-341.

Armitage, R., Hoffmann, R., Fitch T., Trivedi, M. and Rush A. J. (2000). Temporal characteristics of delta activity during NREM sleep in depressed outpatients and healthy adults: group and sex effects. *Sleep.*, *23*, 607-617.

Bangasser, D. A. (2013). Sex Differences in Stress-Related Receptors: "micro" differences with "macro" implications for mood and anxiety disorders. *Biol. Sex. Differ.*, *4*, 2-15.

Barlow, D. H. (2002). *Anxiety and its Disorders: the Nature and Treatment of Anxiety and Panic*. 2nd edn., Guilford Press, New York, 704 pp.

Bastien, C. H., St-Jean, G., Morin, Ch. M., Turcotte, I. and Carrier, J. (2008). Chronic psychophysiological insomnia: hyperarousal and/or inhibition deficits? An ERPs Investigation. *Sleep.*, *31*, 887-898.

Beck, A. T., Emery, G. and Greenberg, R. L. (1985). *Anxiety Disorders and Phobias: a Cognitive Perspective*. Basic Books, New York, 346 pp.

Beck, K. D., Jiao, X., Pang, K. C. H. and Servatius, R. J. (2010). Vulnerability factors in anxiety determined through differences in active-avoidance behavior. Prog. Neuro-Psychopharmacol. *Biol. Psychiatry.*, *34*, 852-860.

Bertolino, A., Arciero, G., Rabino, V., Latorre, V., De Candia, M., Mazzola, V., Blasi, G., Caforio, G., Hariri, A., Kolachana, B., Nardini, M., Weinberger, D. R. and Scarabino, T. (2005). Variation of human amygdala response during threatening stimuli as a function of 5-HTTLPR genotype and personality style. *Biol. Psychiatry.*, *57*, 1517-1525.

Bishop, S. J. (2007). Neurocognitive mechanisms of anxiety: an integrative account. *Trends Cogn. Sci.*, *11*, 307-316.

Bishop, S. J., Duncan, J. and Lawrence, A. D. (2004). State anxiety modulation of the amygdala response to unattended threat-related stimuli. *J. Neurosci.*, *24*, 10364-10368.

Bonnet, M. H. and Arand, D. L. (2010). Hyperarousal and Insomnia: state of the science. *Sleep Med. Rev.*, *19*, 9-15.

Borbely, A. A. (1982). A two process model of sleep regulation. *Hum. Neurobiol.*, *1*, 195-204.

Bradley, B. P., Mogg, K., Falla, J. S. and Hailton, L. R. (1998). Attentional bias for threatening facial expressions in anxiety: manipulation of stimulus duration. *Cogn. Emot.*, *12*, 737-753.

Breslau, N., Davis, G. C., Andreski, P., Peterson, E. L. and Schultz, L. R. (1997). Sex differences in posttraumatic stress disorder. *Arch. Gen. Psychiatry.*, *54*, 1044-1048.

Breslau, N., Roth, T., Rosenthal, L. and Andreski, P. (1996). Sleep disturbance and psychiatric disorders: a longitudinal epidemiological study of young adults. *Biol. Psychiatry.*, *39*. 411-418.

Buechel, H. M., Popovic, J., Searcy, J. L., Porter, N. M., Thibault, O. and Blalock, E. M. (2011). Deep sleep and parietal cortex gene expression changes are related to cognitive deficits with age. *PLoS ONE.*, *6*, e18387-e18398.

Buysse, D. J., Germain, A., Hall, M. L., Moul, D. E., Nofzinger, E. A., Begley, A., Ehlers, C. L., Thompson, W. and Kupfer, D. J. (2008). EEG spectral analysis in primary insomnia: NREM period effects and sex differences. *Sleep.*, *31*, 1673-1682.

Carrier, J., Land, S., Buysse, D. J., Kupfer1, D. J. and Monk, T. H. (2001). The effects of age and gender on sleep EEG power spectral density in the middle years of life (ages 20–60 years old). *Psychophysiol.*, *38*, 232-242.

Cattell, R. B., Eber, H. W. and Tatsuoka, M. M. (1970). *Handbook for the Sixteen Personality Factor Questionnaire*. Champaign, IL: Institute for Personality and Ability Testing.

Catuzzi, J. E. and Beck, K. D. (2014). Anxiety vulnerability in women: A two-hit hypothesis. *Exp. Neurol.* http://dx.doi.org/10.1016/j.expneurol. 2014. 01.023.

Chua, P., Krams, M., Tone, I., Passingham, R. and Dolan, R. (1999). A functional anatomy of anticipatory anxiety. *Neuroimage.*, *9*, 563-571.

Clark, D. M. (1999). Anxiety Disorders: why they persist and how to treat them. *Behav. Res. Ther.*, *37*, S5-S27.

Craske, M. G. (2003). *Origins of Phobias and Anxiety Disorders: Why More Women than Men?* Elsevier Ltd, UK, 292 pp.

Davidson, R. J. (1990). Anxiety and affective style: role of the prefrontal cortex and amygdale. *Biol. Psychol.*, *58*, 330-341.

Davis, M. (1992). The Role of the amygdala in fear and anxiety. *Annu. Rev. Neurosci.*, *15*, 353-375.

Dijk, D. J., Beersma, D. G. M. and Bloem, G. M. (1989). Sex differences in the sleep EEG of young adults: visual scoring and spectral analysis. *Sleep.*, *12*, 500-507.

Dijk, D. J., Beersma, D. G. M. and Daan, S. (1987). EEG power density during nap sleep: reflection of an hourglass measuring the duration of prior wakefulness. *J. Biol. Rhythms.*, *2*, 207-219.

Elegulashvily, T. C. (1997). Sindrom apnoe vo sne. Klinicheskaya medicina. *75.*, 64-67.

Everson, H. and Millsar, R. (1991). Isolating gender differences in test anxiety: a confirmatory factor analysis of the Test Anxiety Inventory. *Educ. Psychol. Measur.*, *51*, 243-251.

Eysenck, M. W. (1992). *Anxiety: The Cognitive Perspective.* Lawrence Erlbaum Associates Ltd, U.K., 195 pp.

Feige, B., Baglioni, Ch., Spiegelhalder, K., Hirscher, V., Nissen, Ch. and Riemann, D. (2013). The microstructure of sleep in primary insomnia: An overview and extension. *Int. J. Psychophysiol.*, *89*, 171-180.

Finelli, L. A., Acherman, P. and Borbely, A. A. (2001). Individual "fingerprints" in human sleep EEG topography. *Neuropsychopharmacol.*, *25*, S57-S62.

Frank, M. G., Issa, N. P. and Stryker, M. P. (2001). Sleep enhances plasticity in the developing visual cortex. *Neuron.*, *30*, 275-287.

Gau, S. F. (2000). Neurotism and sleep–related problems in adolescence. *Sleep.*, *23*, 495-502.

Gray, J. A. (1994). *The Nature of Emotion: Fundamental Questions. Three Fundamental Emotion Systems.* Oxford University Press, New York, 181-238 pp.

Heinz, A., Braus, D. F., Smolka, M. N., Wrase, J., Puls, I., Hermann, D., Klein, S., Grüsser, S. M., Flor, H., Schumann, G., Mann, K. and Büchel, Ch. (2004). Amygdala-prefrontal coupling depends on a genetic variation of the serotonin transporter. *Nat. Neurosci.*, *8*, 20-21.

Henniger, M. S., Ohl, F., Hölter, S. M., Weißenbacher, P., Toschi, N., Lörscher, P., Wigger, A., Spanagel, R. and Landgraf, R. (2000). Unconditioned anxiety and social behaviour in two rat lines selectively bred for high and low anxiety-related behaviour. *Behav. Brain Res.*, *111*, 153-163.

Hettema, J. M. (2008). What is the genetic relationship between anxiety and depression? *Am. J. Med. Genet.*, *148*, 140.

Hirshkowitz, M., Hamilton, C. R., Rando, K. C., Bellamy, M., Willams, R. L. and Karacan, I. (1990). State-trait anxiety scores in adults with sleep complaints. *J. Sleep Res.*, *19*, 163.

Hita-Yañez, E., Atienza, M. and Cantero, J. N. (2013). Polysomnographic and subjective sleep markers of mild cognitive impairment. *Sleep.*, *36*, 1327-1334.

Huber, R., Tononi, G. and Cirelli, Ch. (2006). Exploratory behavior, cortical BDNF expression, and sleep homeostasis. *Sleep.*, *30*, 129-139.

Iber, C., Ancoli-Israel, S., Chesson, A. and Quan, S. F. (2007). *The AASM Manual for the Scoring of Sleep and Associated Events: rules, terminology and technical specifications.* American Academy of Sleep Medicine, Westchester, Illinois, 59 pp.

Jha, S. K., Jones, B. E., Coleman, T., Steinmetz, N., Law, Ch. T., Griffin, G., Hawk, J., Dabbish, N., Kalatsky, V. A. and Frank, M. G. (2005). Sleep-dependent plasticity requires cortical activity. *J. Neurosci.*, *25*, 9266-9274.

Johns, M. W. (1991). A new method for measuring daytime sleepiness: the Epworth sleepiness scale. *Sleep.*, *14*, 540-545.

Killgore, W. D. S. (2013). Self-reported sleep correlates with prefrontal-amygdala functional connectivity and emotional functioning. *Sleep.*, *36*, 1597-1608.

Kim, M. J. and Whalen, P. J. (2009). The structural integrity of an amygdala-prefrontal pathway predicts trait anxiety. *J. Neurosci.*, *29*, 1614-11618.

Klimesch, W. (1999). EEG alpha and theta oscillations reflect cognitive and memory performance: a review and analyze. *Brain Res. Rev.*, *29*, 169-195.

Knyazev, G. G., Savostyanov, A. N. and Levin, E. A. (2006). Alpha synchronization and anxiety: Implication for inhibition vs. alertness hypotheses. *Int. J. Psychophysiol.*, *59*, 151-158.

Koo, J. W., Han, J. S. and Kim, J. J. (2004). Selective neurotoxic lesions of basolateral and central nuclei of the amygdale produce differential effects on fear conditioning. *J. Neurosci.*, *24*, 7654-7662.

Kovrov, G. V. and Vein, A. M. (2004). *Stress I Son U Cheloveka (Stress and Sleep in Humans)*, Neiromedia, Moscow, 183 pp.

Krömer, S. A., Keßler, M. S. and Milfay, D. (2005). Turck identification of glyoxalase-I as a protein marker in a mouse model of extremes in trait anxiety. *J. Neurosci.*, *25*, 4375-4384.

Leger, D., Guilleminault, C., Dreyfus, J. P., Delahaye, C. and Paillard, M. (2009). Prevalence of insomnia in a survey of 12.778 adults in France. *J. Sleep Res.*, *9*, 35-42.

Lindberg, E., Janson, Ch., Gislason, Th., Björnsson, E., Hetta, J. and Boman, G. (1997). Sleep Disturbances in a young adult population: can gender differences be explained by differences in psychological status? *Sleep.*, *20*, 381-387.

Martin-Soelch, Ch., Stöcklin, M., Dammann, G., Opwis, K. and Seifritz, E. (2006). Anxiety trait modulates psychophysiological reaction, but not habituation processes related to affective auditory stimuli. *Int. J. Psychophysiol.*, *61*, 87-97.

Matthews, G., Panganiban, A. R. and Hudlicka, E. (2011). Anxiety and selective attention to threat in tactical decision-making. *Personal. Individ. Differ.*, *50*, 949-954.

McEvoy, L. K., Pellouchoud, E., Smith, M. E. and Gevins, A. (2001). Neurophysiological signals of working memory in normal aging. *Brain Res. Cogn. Brain Res.*, *11*, 363-376.

McLean, C. P. and Anderson, E. R. (2009). Brave men and timid women? A review of the gender differences in fear and anxiety. *Clin. Psychol. Rev.*, *29*, 496-505.

McNally, R. J. (1982). Information – processing abnormalities in anxiety disoders: implications for cognitive neuroscience. *Cogn. Emot.*, *12*, 479-495.

Nebylitsin, V. D. (1966). *Osnovnye svoistva nervnoy sistemy cheloveka*, Prosvezhenie, Moskow, 289 pp.

Nebylitsin, V. D. (2000). *Problemy psychologii individualnosti. Izbrannye psichologicheskie trudy*, Izdatelstvo NPO "MODEK," Moskow, 688 pp.

Phelps, E. A., O'Conner, K. J., Gatenby, J. C., Gore, J. C., Grillon, C. and Davis, M. (2001). Activation of the left amygdala to a cognitive representation of fear. *Nat. Neurosci.*, *4*, 437-441.

Putman, P. (2011). Resting state EEG delta–beta coherence in relation to anxiety, behavioral inhibition, and selective attentional processing of threatening stimuli. *Int. J. Psychophysiol.*, *80*, 63-68.

Rechtschaffen, A. and Kales, A. A. (1968). *Manual of standardized terminology, techniques and scoring system for sleep stages of human subjects*. University of California, Brain Information Service/Brain Research Institute, Los Angeles, CA.

Reynolds, C. F., Kupfer, D. J., Thase, T., Frank, E., Jarrett, D. B., Coble, P. A., Hoch, C. C., Buysse, D. J., Simons, A. D. and Houck, P. R. (1990). Sleep, gender, and depression: an analysis of gender effects on the electroencephalographic sleep of 302 depresses outpatients. *Biol. Psychiatry.*, *28*, 673-684.

Roehrs, T., Timms, V. and Zwyghuizen-Doorenbos, A. (1990). Polysomnographic performance and personality differences of sleepy and alert normals. *Sleep.*, *13*, 395-402.

Rosa, R. R., Bonnet, M. H. and Kramer, M. (1983). The relationship of sleep and anxiety in anxious subjects. *Biol. Psychol.*, *16*, 119-126.

Rusalov, V. M. (1979). *Biologicheskie Osnovy Individualno-Psichologicheskih Raslichiy*. Nauka, Moskow, 328 pp.

Sandi, C. and Richter-Levin, G. (2009). From high anxiety trait to depression a neurocognitive hypothesis. *Trends Neurosci.*, *32*, 312-320.

Savost'ianov, A. N. and Savost'ianova, D. A. (2003). Changes in brain electrical activity during habituation to verbal stimulus in subjects with high and low anxiety. *Zh. Vyssh. Nerv. Deyat. I.P. Pavlova.*, *53*, 351-360.

Sheynina, J., Becka, K. D., Panga, K. C. H., Servatiusa, R. J., Shikarid, S., Ostovichd, J. and Myersa, C. E. (2014). Behaviorally inhibited temperament and female sex, two vulnerability factors for anxiety disorders, facilitate conditioned avoidance (also) in humans. *Behav. Processes.*, *103*, 228-235.

Shin, L. M., Whalen, P. J., Pitman, R. K., Bush, G., Macklin, M. L., Lasko, N. B., Orr, S. P., McInerney, S. C. and Rauch S. L. (2001). An fMRI study of anterior cingulate function in posttraumatic stress disorder. *Biol. Psychiatry.*, *50*, 932-942.

Spielberger, Ch. D. (1985). Assessment of state and trait anxiety: conceptual and methodological issues. *South. Psychol.*, *2*, 6-10.

St-Jean, G., Turcotte, I., Pérusse, A. D. and Bastien, C. H. (2013). REM and NREM power spectral analysis on two consecutive nights in psychophysiological and paradoxical insomnia sufferers. *International. J. Psychophysiol.*, *89*, 181-194.

Sysoeva, Yu. Yu. (2008). Influence Anxiety on Structure and EEG-parameters of the Nighttime Sleep. *In. Sleep and Anxiety*, edited by E.V. Verbitsky. SSC RAS, Rostov-on-Don, 174-186.

Tan, J., Ma, Z., Gao, X., Wu, Y. and Fang, F. (2011). Gender difference of unconscious attentional bias in high trait anxiety individuals. *PLoS ONE.*, *6*, e20305-e20311.

Taylor, J. A. (1953). A personality scale of manifest anxiety. *J. Abnorm. Soc. Psychol.*, *48*, 285-290.

Teplov, B. M. (1961). *Problemy Individualnych razlichiy.* Academia pedagogicheskih nauk RSFSR, Moskow, 302 s.

Tononi, G. and Cirelli, Ch. (2001). Modulation of brain gene expression during sleep and wakefulness: a review of recent findings. *Neuropsychopharmacol.*, *25*, S28-S35.

Tononi, G. and Cirelli, Ch. (2003). Sleep and sleep homeostasis: a hypothesis. *Brain Res. Bull.*, *62*, 143-150.

Tononi, G. and Cirelli, Ch. (2006). Sleep function and synaptic homeostasis. *Sleep Med. Rev.*, *10*, 49-54.

Turcotte, I. and Bastien, C. H. (2009). Is quality of sleep related to the N1 and P2 ERPs in chronic psychophysiological insomnia sufferers? *Int. J. Psychophysiol.*, *72*, 314-322.

Vahtera, J., Kivimäki, M., Hublin, Ch., Korkeila, K., Suominen, S., Paunio, T. and Koskenvuo, M. (2007). Liability to anxiety and severe life events as predictors of new-onset sleep disturbances. *Sleep.*, *30*, 1537-1546.

Van Dongen, H. P. A., Maislin, G., Mullington, J. M. and Dinges, D. F. (2003). The cumulative cost of additional wakefulness: dose-response effects on neurobehavioral functions and sleep physiology from chronic sleep restriction and total sleep deprivation. *Sleep.*, *2*, 117-126.

Veldhuizen, R. J., Jonkman, E. J. and Poortvliet, D. C. J. (1993). Sex differences in age regression parameters of healthy adults – normative data and practical implications. Electroencephalogr. *Clin. Neurophysiol.*, *86*, 377-384.

Veyn, A. M. and Hecht, K. (1989). Son cheloveca. Fisiologia i patologia. Medizina, Moskow, 267 s.

Vuilleumeier, P. (2002). Facial expression and selective attention. *Curr. Opin. Psychiatry.*, *15*, 291-300.

Walentowska, W. and Wronka, E. (2012). Trait anxiety and involuntary processing of facial emotions. *Int. J. Psychophysiol.*, *85*, 27-36.

Williams, L. M., Simms, E., Clark, C. R., Paul, R. H., Rowe, D. and Gordon, E. (2005). The test-retest reliability of a standardized neurocognitive and neurophysiological test battery: "neuromarker." *Int. J Neurosci.*, *115*, 1605-1630.

Willmann, M., Langlet, C., Hainaut, J. Ph. and Bolmont, B. (2012). The time course of autonomic parameters and muscle tension during recovery following a moderate cognitive stressor: dependency on trait anxiety level. *Int. J. Psychophysiol.*, *84*, 51-58.

Zigmond, A. S. and Snaith, R. P. (1983). The hospital anxiety and depression scale. *Acta Psychiatrica Scandinavica.*, *67*, 361-370.

BIOGRAPHICAL SKETCH

Name: Yulia Arapova (former surname Sysoeva)

Affiliation: Department of Physiology, Institute of Arid Zones of the Southern Scientific Center, Institution of the Russian Academy of Science

Date of Birth: November 28, 1978; Rostov-on-Don, USSR

Education: PhD in Biology (Neuroscience and Neurophysiology) 2008, Astrakhan State University, Russia

Thesis title: "The Study of Relationship of Personal Anxiety and Electrophysiological Parameters of the Night Sleep."

PhD student in Biology 2004 - 2007, Kogan Research Inst. for Neurocybernetics, Rostov State University, Russia.

Graduate student (biologist adequacy) in Biology (Physiology of Man and Animal): 1996 - 2003, Department of Human and Animals Physiology, Faculty of Biology and Soil,Rostov State University, Rostov-on-Don, Russia

Thesis title: "The Influence of Morphoanatomical Characteristics on the Development of Non-Volitional and Volitional Attention in Preschoolers."

Address: 41, Chekhov str.
344006 Rostov-on-Don,
Russia

Research and Professional Experience: December 2010 – present: Researcher, Scientific Group for Physiology, Institute of Arid Zones of Southern Scientific Center of Russian Academy of Science, Rostov-on-Don, Russia.

- The studies of sleep-wakefulness cycle of human on norm and pathology (obstructive sleep apnea, anxiety, insomnia in adults and children)
- The studies of gender differences of daily and night sleep in aspect of anxiety.
- The studies of neurophysiologic mechanisms of personal reactivity that is necessary for adaptation of mammals in arid zone during sleep-wakefulness cycle.
- The research of sleep-wakefulness changes during adaptation to high altitude.

Polysomnology. Electrophysiological recordings of SCN activity (spontaneous neuronal activity; evoked potentials), EEG, breathing rate, EMG and other physiological parameters on humans.

December 2008 – December 2010: Researcher, Scientific Group for Physiology, Southern Scientific Center of Russian Academy of Science, Rostov-on-Don, Russia.

Neurophysiological mechanisms of personal anxiety in sleep-wakefulness cycle. Polysomnology. Electrophysiological recordings of SCN activity (spontaneous neuronal activity), EEG, breathing rate, EMG and other physiological parameters on humans.

August 2003 – November 2008: Junior Researcher, Department of Processes of SNC and behavioral management, Kogan Res. Inst. for Neurocybernetics, Rostov State Univ., Russia.

- The influence of level of personal anxiety on organization of sleep-wakefulness cycle (object of research is humans)
- Electrophysiological study of cortical-subcortical interaction during sleep (on cats). (differentiation on level of anxiety, spontaneous neuronal activity; evoked potentials induced by vibroacoustic stimulation).

September 2001 - August 2003: Laboratory assistant, Laboratory of Clinical Immunology, Municipal Hospital № 20, Rostov-on-Don, Russia.

- The immunological status of pregnant women

Professional Appointments:

psychophysiology, somnology, electrophysiology

Honors:

2008 – Governor's Award for outstanding ability in scientific activity

2015. – Honorary Citation of the Institute of Arid Zones of the Southern Scientific Center, Institution of the Russian Academy of Science

Publications Last 3 Years:

1. Yu. Yu. Sysoeva and E. V. Verbitsky, 2013. Influence of the Level of Trait Anxiety on Sleep EEG of Men and Women. Human Physiology. Vol. 39, No. 6, pp. 655–662.
2. Yu. Yu. Sysoeva, E.V. Verbitsky, 2015. Characteristics of Sleep-Related Arousals Depend on Trait Anxiety. Doklady Biological Sciences. Vol. 461, pp. 1–3.
3. Sysoeva Yu. Yu., Verbitsky E.V. The gender differences and anxiety in concept of sleep. Proceedings of the 7th International Workshop "Sleep: a window to the world of wakefulness." October 10-12, 2013. Rostov-on-Don, Russia. P. 57.
4. Arapova Yu. Yu., Verbitsky E.V. A Conception of the brain activation in sleep-wakefulness cycle and personal anxiety. XI International interdisciplinary congress Neuroscience for medicine and psychology. Sudak, Crimea, Russia, June 2-12, 2015. p. 61-62.
5. Arapova Yu. Yu.,Verbitsky E.V. Age-related features of sleep at early childhood proceedings Of the 8th International Youth Workshop "Sleep: a window to the world of wakefulness" May 14-16, 2015.

INDEX

A

B

C

D

E

F

G

H

I

L

M

Q

R

T

U

V

W

Y